TOURIST GUIDE • USEFUL INFORMATION • MAP

SANTORINI

© ADAM EDITIONS-PERGAMOS S.A., KATSIMICHA, 190 02 PEANIA-ATTICA
TEL: 210 6644514-5, FAX: 210 6644512, e-mail.: pergamos@adam-editions.gr

TOURIST GUIDE • USEFUL INFORMATION • MAP

SANTORINI

Santorini, a unique place

ADAM EDITIONS

CONTENTS

Queen of the Aegean pulse and wing

You have found the words to convert infinity

With fire lava and smoke

The great line of your destiny...

A passage from "Ode to Santorini"
by Odysseas Elytis

The unique "figure" of Santorini emerges magical,

attractive and unexpected

from the Aegean deep blue.

A shape so different from the rest of the Cyclades Islands!

The volcano has left indelible marks

on its land and has created an idiosyncratic landscape

which attests to the island's eventful history.

At the same time this uniqueness of nature

has rendered it universally known, popular and cherished.

SANTORINI,
A UNIQUE PLACE

 Santorini is one of the many Cyclades Islands with which the Aegean Sea is studded; an island that during the last decades with its picturesque character and beauty inspired numerous artists, among them well-known painters, photographers and writers.

The poets and Nobel Prize winners George Seferis and Odysseas Elytis praised its unsurpassable presence. Dimitris Vasiliadis exalted the creations of its popular architecture while the Academic Elias Venezis admired them because they are made with modesty and harmony. The famous Greek photographer Nelly's felt enchanted and with her sensibility immortalized the unique plasticity of the houses, the lyric atmosphere of the landscape and the simplicity of the inhabitants.

The writer I. M. Panagiotopoulos called it "the wounded island". He saw it as another world which "... belongs to the peculiarities, the oddities, the paradoxes of the Greek landscape". And he added "... all this white, as the sun makes it shine, as the Cycladic summer sets it on fire, transforms the island into a huge seabird that sways happily inside the absolute blue, light and serene waters of the world. The island's little towns are covered by shadowy cellars and arched pebble-paved streets. Therein the burning body receives freshness and tranquility".

The wildness of the idiosyncratic Skaros is smoothed by the whiteness of the houses and the azure of the Aegean.

Santorini's idiosyncratic nature, which is the result of the age-long volcanic activity, has become the object of geological studies (the existing volcano is one of the most studied volcanoes –after Vesuvio) while the important finds that have been uncovered in its soil attract the interest of historians and archaeologists alike.

Santorini is a unique place. Lacerated beyond repair by the fury of elements, it stands up against adversities and endows those born on its soil with unequalled vigour and strength. At the same time, it provides them with everything necessary so as to live with dignity.

In the past, its inhabitants used to rely for their livelihood, on the exploitation of volcanic materials, which abound on the island. Thus, for many years, long before tourism became an important sector of local economy, these rocks (or porcelana as locals call them) which were used for insulation and submarine constructions constituted the most important income source for the island. Moreover, its soil because of its volcanic nature produced goods in small quantities but of an excellent quality. So the volcano during the difficult survival struggle of the island did not leave behind only scorched earth but also certain goods.

Nowadays, everything is different. In Santorini, the swift development

The sunsets in Oea are fascinating. As the sun prepares to "dive" into the waters, the Aegean looks as if it is "set alight".

of the tourist sector during the last decades has had as a result the radical change of life for the locals as compared to the 50s. Currently, it is a modern tourist resort, which has developed swiftly. Every year it swarms with countless visitors. Nonetheless, it manages to preserve its beauty and its picturesque character. The Santorini sunsets are unique and fascinating. The coast opposite the volcano, grey or reddish in some places and blackish in others, falls into the blue sea. The white shapes of the houses hang on the edge of the caldera precipice (the basin, that reaches a depth of 390m.). They look as if they stare at the infinity of the Aegean and, as the boat approaches, resemble marks of light on the dark stone. They try to hitch on a stone, a thorn, on the abyss, with the most dangerous means and they succeed very graciously, writes the painter N. Chadjikyriakos – Ghikas.

Its beaches with the grey-black volcanic sand offer a totally different picture than that of the other Cyclades islands.

Santorini is indeed unique. It is time to get to know it!

LAND, LANDSCAPE, PEOPLE

The island, which has inspired artists and writers, lies between Ios and Anafi and is one of the most southerly Cyclades islands. It is also called Thera and is a province of the Prefecture of Cyclades.

Its distance from Piraeus is 130 nautical miles and from Crete only 70 nautical miles. Its land area is 93 square kilometers and its coastline 69 kilometers. Its length from north (Mavropetra cape) to south (Exomitis cape) is 18 kilometers while its width varies from 2 to 6 kilometers. Its highest peak is Prophet Elias (566 meters), while there are some lower ones (Megalo Vouno, Small Prophet Elias etc.).

Santorini has a population of approximately 7,000 who live in 13 villages (Thera or Fira, Akrotiri, Vothonas, Vourvoulos, Emborio or Niborio,

The houses of Oea, the other large settlement of Santorini, built on the tip of the caldera, look like acrobats "balancing" on the edge of the cliff.

Exo Gonia, Episkopi Gonias or Mesa Gonia, Imerovigli, Karterados, Megalochori, Mesaria, Oea, Pyrgos). Fira is the capital and Athinios is its harbour.

On the west the island's coastline sinks from great heights (from 200 to 300 meters) steeply into the sea, into the waters of the circular caldera which has a surface of 82,5 square kilometers and depths of 300-390 meters. It is estimated that the caldera was created between 1700 and 1600 BC, when Strongyli, the island which was lying until then on the site of contemporary Santorini, was broken into pieces as a result of a powerful eruption of the volcano which was rising at its central part. A great part of Strongyli sunk into the sea and what was left of this immersion, except Santorini, were the islands of Theresia and uninhabited Aspronisi which complete the circular contour of the old island. Seawater flooded the empty space, which was created after the prehistoric immersion, and in this way the basin was formed. According to the international terminology, the basin is called caldera, and at its centre lie the Palea and Nea Kameni islets that were created by submarine volcanic flows in later periods.

The dark mass of the caldera's inner side with the white houses hanging literally above the abyss offer a breathtaking view to the visitor star-

The capital, the all white Fira also built on the edge of the cliff contemplates the dark shape of Nea Kameni. Its architecture in combination with the fascinating landscape and the unique view of the volcano make Fira a breathtaking site.

ing at Santorini for the first time. Here, on the edge and along the precipice the Fira, Firostefano, Imerovigli and Oea settlements have been developed.

The caldera steep slopes, besides the wonderful landscape they offer to the visitor of the island, also constitute a unique intersection for the study of the volcanic and geologic character of the soil. The various volcanic strata are distinguished thanks to their colours, which range from red to black. And above all these rocks lies the thick stratum of pumice-stone and ashes, with a thickness reaching 40 meters. The exploitation of these two rocks, which can be used as insulation materials, constituted for years the mainstay of the island's economy, as it is calculated that until recently more than 2,000,000 tons of pumice and ash were exported every year. The other side of the island, which looks eastwards to the open sea, ends in an unusually fertile level plain with low vegetation. The cause of its fertility is the volcanic soil, which is so soft, almost fragments of lava, that it has the quality to hold the rain humidity and the atmospheric dew.

Santorini is famous for its delicious and excellent quality products. Wines, split peas, white eggplants, cucumbers and tomatoes are among them.

The Santorini climate is pleasant, mild and humid. Northern and north-eastern winds blow often (the well-known meltemia –yearly winds) and moderate the summer heat.

Fishing-nets are getting ready for the next fishing.

Its inhabitants are simple and hospitable. In the past, their main occupations besides sea-faring were unusual for islanders: agriculture and quarrying of volcanic rocks. This was the result of the distance between their settlements (Fira, Oea, Karte-rados, Mesaria) from the sea. Only the inhabitants of Niborio were fishermen. Nowadays, the professional occupations of the inhabitants are mainly tourism-related, as this sector consti-tutes the mainstay of the island's economy. However, from the above-mentioned agricultural products vineyards are sys-tematically cropped for the pro-duction of wine. Santorini is

Houses and streets in Fira follow the configuration of the soil. They look as if they are intermingled into a hopeless effort of finding some free space while between the terraces, in the yards and vaults the characteristic shape of the St. Menas church is distinguished.

currently one of the principal poles of attraction in Greece and one of the country's greatest tourist resorts, both due to the two important civilizations (Akrotiri, Ancient Thera) which were brought to light by excavations and to its unusual natural beauty. The island is connected by sea with Piraeus and other Aegean islands and by air with Athens, some other Greek regions and foreign countries.

The cruiseships, which arrive at Santorini, moor in the almost circular basin of the caldera, off Mesa Yalos. High on the edge of the cliff appear the all white houses of Fira as if they are hanging on the rock.

SANTORINI, PAST AND PRESENT

Santorini is a narrow strip of land, a tiny island, and its inhabitants were accustomed to fight hard all along in order to provide for their livelihood. The island is arid and although the soil is fertile and its products are of a good quality they did not suffice to feed them. Therefore, from the early years some inhabitants turned to the sea. They became seamen and traders and started to trade products, such as wine, outside the island.

During the 17th, 18th, and 19th centuries, foreign travellers, usually French and English, who travelled in the Aegean, visited Santorini. Reading today their precious testimonies and narratives we can discover many interesting data for the island, the volcanic eruptions, and the inhabitants and their hard fight for survival. One of these travellers was the French clergyman François Richard who lived many years in Santorini. In his chronicle, which was published in Paris in 1675, he speaks about the island's castles, its products, inhabitants, their alimentary habits and their faith. From the information he offers we learn that in 1650 Santorini had 7,000 inhabitants. The great majority of them were Orthodox and only 700 were Catholics. On the island there were approximately 300 churches. That is to say that there was one church for every 20 inhabitants. The local people had a deep faith in the Virgin Mary. They considered her as mother, landlady and guardian of their homes. This infinite devotion was visible in every moment of daily life. The Virgin Mary was present both in churches and homes (her icon decorated every household and housewives lighted an oil-lamp on Saturday evening) and in language, prayers and deeds.

Original all white bell-towers and asure domes, works of local craftsmen, decorate the Santorini churches.

More than 50 of the island churches were dedicated to her. But even in churches dedicated to other saints her icon was always present and those entering the temple genuflected before her icon. They vowed to the Virgin Mary when they wanted to take a sacred vow, asked for help when adversities occurred, and through her thanked God. They never set forth a journey without promising a votive offering to her, and almost everybody left part of his belongings to one of the churches bearing her name.

Moreover, the French traveller speaks about the lack of water in Santorini where there are neither torrents nor springs. Therefore the inhabitants used to collect the rainwater into cisterns. If there was not enough precipitation, then the soil became parched and the inhabitants resorted to the brack-

The great number of churches on the island is due to the intense religious feeling of its inhabitants. The artisans draw inspiration from their faith to the divine and unsurpassed landscape of their island and manage to create small masterpieces.

Women of Santorini (Choiseul-Gouffier).

Vendema was for the inhabitants the feast of the plain. Female workers having their heads covered by scarves so as to protect them from the sun put the grapes into large baskets and brought them to the canava

(Nik. N. Nomikos).

ish water of the wells situated near the beaches. Nonetheless, whatever crop was farmed on the island was of excellent quality. How did this happen? How was it possible with so little water to produce such excellent crops? From where did the soil receive the necessary water? From the dew which it absorbed drop by drop in the night.

During the years that François Richard visited Santorini, barley was farmed on the island, with which the local people used to make bread, which in its turn was made into rusks. In addition, they produced millet, sesame, beans, and cucumbers, which were called "katzokia", big and juicy melons and fresh peas, which were cooked into a delicious mash. Finally, most of the wine was sold to Russia while a part of it was sold to Chios, Smyrna and even Constantinople. The local people's diet was frugal (See below, the Local Cuisine, p. 135). The barley rusks were wetted and were accompanied by salted quails that were caught during the hunting season. Besides this combination, they usually ate vegetables. Only the rich could afford to eat meat, mainly beef, which was the product of animals slaughtered once a year; the meat after being salted with salt and vinegar was left to dry under the sun for 7-8 days, in order to preserve it for a long period. This salted meat was cooked, baked or simply eaten as it was.

Next to the cattlebreeding, poultry was also raised and fed with the abundant barley farmed on the island.

The local people's diet also included game and seafood. When the migratory birds stopped on the island during the autumn, hundreds of quails and turtledoves were caught. Fishing was an occupation which started in autumn and went on until May. The most common species fished was a kind of sardine called "gripas". The precious information given by François Richard is completed with references to the women's costumes (used to wear short dresses barely reaching the knee), and to events that show the superstitions of the inhabitants.

In 1666 a bishop called Sebastiani is touring through the Mediterranean. He visits Santorini, about which he writes that it is known as the "island of the demons" or "the island of hell". These were names given to the island by his contemporaries, obviously because of the volcanic eruptions. The fact that the boat skippers cannot reach the sea bottom for anchorage is considered strange. Thus stories are made up about demons that cut the boats' anchors and as a result cannot moor in the harbour.

A few years later, in 1675, an English traveller this time, called Bernard Randolph, sets foot in Santorini and informs us that the local traders bought the spoil of pirates which was then transported and sold in Smyrna. There, they bought cotton for the island's looms that produced the best cotton textiles in the Aegean.

The passing of time brought little change to the island. The conquerors left. During the 20th century some of the inhabitants made fortunes from seafaring and trade. But the majority of those left on the island continued their fight for survival. Their main occupation besides the quarrying of pumice was agriculture. Wine, tomatoes, split peas, barley and caper were the basic products.

The inhabitants did not proceed to tread the grapes on the same day they were harvested, but on the contrary they piled them in the winepress until the vine-harvest was completed. Only then they treaded them. This accumulated mass tinged the grapes and as a result the Santorini wine, even the white one, has an intense colour.

There were two kinds of "brusco" (dry wine), white and red. The white one was not completely white but it had a mild cinnamon tone and was the product of Asirtika grapes. The "nichteri" wine, which was even whiter than the resinated wine was the product of grapes that were treaded upon harvest, while the table grapes produced "malavasias", which is also called nectar of Santorini. The sweet "visanto", etymologically derived from vino santo (it means sacred wine, wine used for the Holy Communion), was made of grapes which were left to "toast" under the sun. Besides the sweet "visanto" there was also the semi-sweet mezzo, for the production of which they used half must from fresh grapes and half from "toasted" ones.

Another habit of the local people that it is preserved until today is to prune the vines on parched soil very short in order to protect them from long dry spells. They also usually twine the trunks in a basket-like manner in order to protect them from the winds.

WINES

Santorini was always famous for its excellent wines, such as "nichteri", "brusco", "malavazias" and "visanto". Thirty-six varieties of grapes were farmed on the

island. From these, the Asirtiko (a white variety farmed until now) and Mandilaria (a black one) were used for the production of wine while all the rest which were in any case scant, were table grapes. From the last group, the Aidania variety was used as well for the production of wine.

Mesaria is built on a fertile plain, farmed with vines where the greatest part of the local wine is produced. →

The "vedema" as the grape-harvest is called in Santorini, began after the 15th of August and was more than a joyful event; it was a feast that lasted many days. It started with the preparations, which included the cleaning and painting of the "kanava" (wine factory) and its implements, the cleaning of the "liastra", that is the terrace on which the grapes were left to dry, the arrangement for the transportation of the big baskets with the grapes (by horse or donkey) from the fields to the wine-presses and the agreements with the workers who were needed for the grape-harvest. On the eve of the feast of Dormition of the Virgin Mary (15th of August), the preparations were completed and the church's bells in Niborio, which was the first village of the island to start with the harvest, gave the signal that the vedema was about to start. Joyful voices livened up the narrow streets and fields. The workers worked incessantly. The animals were loaded with big baskets full of ripe delicious fruits. They transported them through narrow streets. They were unloaded outside the wine factory and then the drivers emptied them into the winepresses, different ones for the white and black grapes. And the day went on. In the evening the kanava yard was still bursting with joy and the workers' voices. They ate and drank together while resting from the day's hard work. In the end, when they were in high spirits, someone played the lyre or tsabouna (bagpipes) and they started to sing and dance. They danced "repati" and made improvised couplets to tease the boss, friends or to flirt with a girl. A big celebration took place upon conclusion of the vedema. During the next morning they started treading the grapes, an event also accompanied by musical instruments that were, besides lyre and bagpipes, violin, lute and clarinet.

After treading, the must from the winepress was put into the "voutsia" (barrels) where the fermentation process began and which lasted until the St. Averkios day, that is the 22nd of October. Then the inhabitants of Niborio opened the barrels and tasted the wine.

It seems that tomatoes, which are small but very tasty, have been farmed

SPLIT PEAS

Besides wine, well known until today are the Santorini split peas, which are produced from a fresh-peas variety farmed on the island.

They were sowed in November or December and harvested between May and June. They were rooted up manually very early in the morning before sunrise. Then they were carried to the threshing floor. There, after threshing the ears they winnowed the chaff from the peas. Next, they sifted the peas through a big iron riddle in order to separate them from stones and dung and whatever chaffs were left over. Finally, they kept it in large wooden trunks. The housewives took the peas from the trunks; they cleaned them carefully and put them into the hand-mill. The hand-mill had two millstones, one above the other, with a hole in the middle for the wooden handle. The peas passed through the hole and were crushed. Thus one of the tastier specialties of the local cuisine, the split peas were ready to be cooked in the earthen pot with oil and onions (See p. 135).

in Santorini since 1920. Tomato farming was soon widespread because it was more profitable than vine farming. The tomatoes were sowed in March. In May, the premature tomatoes called primarolia were harvested while in the end of June the small vedema started. From this variety of tomatoes which were called koumedoria (a corrupted form of the words pommo d'oro) tomato-paste was made, called beltes. At first, the tomato-paste production was primitive. The tomatoes were transported to the drying-field. There, local women crushed them with their bear hands. Then they squeezed them and passed the juice through a big strainer. It was salted and boiled in large coppers, put into troughs and left to dry on the houses' terraces. Finally, it was gathered and kept in barrels. This was the process to make the tomato-paste, which was consumed in the winter. In 1924, when tomato production increased, the first mill was founded in Monolithos and many others followed later. In these mills that today are deserted, the tomatoes were pulped and the paste was put into tins.

The shortly pruned vines on purched soil produced the famous Santorini wine: brusco, nichteri, malavazias, visanto, and sweet mezzo.

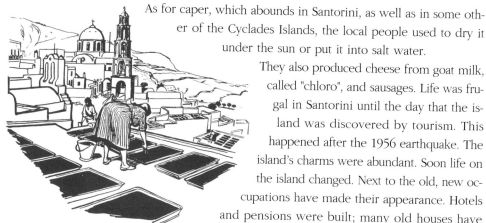

As for caper, which abounds in Santorini, as well as in some other of the Cyclades Islands, the local people used to dry it under the sun or put it into salt water.

They also produced cheese from goat milk, called "chloro", and sausages. Life was frugal in Santorini until the day that the island was discovered by tourism. This happened after the 1956 earthquake. The island's charms were abundant. Soon life on the island changed. Next to the old, new occupations have made their appearance. Hotels and pensions were built; many old houses have been converted into restaurants, bars, cafés, and shops.

Local women put tomato-paste into the kneading-troughs and let it dry under the sun in order for it to be used during the cold winter nights.

(Nik. N. Nomikos).

Several foreigners who came here did not leave and became permanent residents. New settlements have been created while the old ones have expanded. A harbour has been constructed for the mooring of ships and therefore the passengers do not have to approach Mesa Yalos by boat. A funicular railway has been constructed for the transportation of passengers from the harbour to Fira or from Fira to Yalos. Gradually, Santorini has changed and adapted to the new conditions that have been created by the numerous tourists who visit it every year. The pace of life has changed. A great distance separates the present from the past. But once in a while, some pictures such as the loaded donkey that ascends the cobbled road, the workers who liven up the vineyards with their voices during the grape-harvest or the believers on Saturday night before Easter who come out of the churches with their improvised hand lanterns lit and flood the quiet and dark streets bring sweet memories from the past.

The landscape of Fira contributed to its emergence as an important tourist resort.

T H E   V O L C A N O

If we trace back to the distant past, we will find out that the creation of Santorini is the result of volcanic activity, which lasted entire milleniums. In the beginning, where now Greece lies, there was sea. In this sea, after cosmogonical eruptions that took place in the depths of the earth approximately 30,000,000 years ago, a unified piece of land stretching from the Ionian Sea to Asia Minor and Crete's southern coasts was created; it was called Aegeida. On its surface rose many mountain ranges with valleys and lakes. In the course of time, Aegeida was cut into pieces and as a result Europe was separated from Asia. In its section, which is currently covered by the Aegean Sea, only the higher summits remained; in the course of time they became the Aegean Islands. The lime rock of Prophet Elias and the semi-crystalline and slate rocks of the region, which is contained between Pyrgos and Mesa Vouno as well as the appendages of Platanimos and Athinios, it seems that they were rocky islets on the site of contemporary Santorini while Monolithos during that very remote period was a small reef. Due to the volcanic activity, which was already present in the region 26,000,000 years ago, the islets joined the volcanic craters that emerged from the sea and created a big island with a total area of approximately 103 square kilometers which, according to Herodotus, was called Strongyli (Greek for round) because of its form. The centre of this round island, according to the researchers' conclusions, was dominated by a volcanic cone approximately 1,000 meters high, on the summit of which a crater must have lain while other smaller craters were situated on its slopes. Burning lava used to fling from the volcano's mouths and roll to the sea. In the course of time, the volcano was extinguished and after thousands of years vegetation and life appeared on the island.

Around 3000 BC, as newer research shows, a powerful eruption of the volcano shook Santorini while its most important activity dates from some centuries later, around the end of the 17th century BC (approximately 1650 BC). The eruption of that period must have been terrifying. It seems that the fling of materials from the cone created a huge vacuum inside the volcano that had as a result the collapse of the interior upper part and the circular landslide of the soil.

The central part of the island of a total area bigger the 83m² collapsed into the sea and the water covered the abyss, which was created with an initial depth of 800 meters. Thus, the biggest caldera in the world was created. From the prehistoric Strongyli, only Santorini, Therasia and Aspronisi remained. According to the estimations of re-

Plan of Santorini where the dotted line shows the area occupied by Strongyli before the prehistoric volcanic eruption around the end of the 17th century BC, an eruption which led to its breaking into three smaller islands: contemporary Santorini, Therasia, and Aspronisi.

searchers who have studied the phenomenon, the eruption and collapse must have been followed by huge tidal waves that hit the Aegean costs, a view also shared by Spiros Marinatos.

Newer geological research in the Ammoudaras region has located deposits of sea sand, which are typical of tidal waves. These waves which hit the northern Cretan coasts must have been about 10 meters high and had the power to destroy any coastal facilities. Consequently, if the hypothesis that the volcanic centre of Santorini produced the tidal wave during the 17th century BC is proven, then it is possible that the volcanic eruption influenced the Minoan Crete.

The Pharaoh's plagues were perhaps the results of the lethal gazes which were unleashed from the volcano and were brought to Egypt by the winds, while myths from Attica, Argolis and Lycea including the myth of Hercules and the three-Hesperus night speak about huge floods and destruction and must have been attempts to interpret the natural phenomena that accompanied the eruption.

Above: Nea Kameni where the crater of the currently 'inactive' volcano lies.

Below, left: In the narrow sea channel that separates Palia and Nea Kameni the petrified lava baths into greenish waters.

Below, right: The barren, yellowish soil of Nea Kameni creates a unique and wild landscape.

ATLANTIS, THE LOST LAND

The prehistoric destruction of Santorini brings to mind the myth about Atlantis, the famous state with the thriving civilization, which sank to the bottom of the sea. Indeed, many believed that Atlantis rests in the Aegean depths and associate Santorini to the mythical state that sank while prospering. Plato was the first to speak about the legendary Atlantis and its civilization in his philosophical dialogues in "Timaeus" and "Critias". The story was told to Critias by his homonymous great-grandfather who had heard about it from his father Dropidas who in his turn had heard it from the Athenian legislator Solon. The story was told to Solon by the Sais priests when he visited Egypt, around

The eruption of the Santorini volcano in 1866. Illustrated London News 1866.

590 BC. According to his narrative, Atlantis was an important and brilliant state, which dominated the other islands. Its supremacy was due to its lofty civilization. It was a kingdom consisting of two islands the "major" and the "minor" ones, divided into ten states, only two of which were mentioned: Metropolis and Royal City. Besides the islands around it, it dominated a part of Africa from Libya to Egypt and a part of Europe reaching until Terrene (contemporary Etrouria in North Italy). The attempts of its inhabitants to subdue Egypt, Attica and the entire area inside the Herculean Columns (the Strait of Gibraltar) were frustrated by the Athenians who were the leaders of the Greeks and who succeeded in defeating the invaders and liberated the conquered peoples. During this period disaster came. Terrible earthquakes and floods hit the area and in one day the entire Atlantis sank into the sea. These events, according to the myth, took place 9000 years before Solon.

The way the island of Thera was destroyed brings Atlantis to mind. Thus, the finds of excavations in Akrotiri, the generally accepted correction of the date of sinking, from 9000 to 900 years before Solon and the lack of certainty among scientists as to the exact date of the eruption (the first estimations located the eruption around 1500 BC) led some researchers to the conclusion that the lost Atlantis was no other than the island of Santorini. However, the size of Atlantis and its cultural characteristics do not match those of Thera. Besides, the island that confronted the Mycenean world in mainland Greece was Crete and not Santorini. In view of this, the archaeologist and professor Spiros Marinatos, who conducted excavations in Crete, and who was the first to systematically study Santorini, formulated the following theory. If we want to identify a site with Atlantis this must be Crete, which probably was the "major" island, the "Royal City" while Santorini which was allied to Crete was "Metropolis" the "minor" island. Moreover, according to the theory of Spiros Marinatos, the damages sustained by the Minoan palace because of the Santorini volcanic eruptions must have been extensive. Seemingly, a tidal wave hit the Cretan coasts. The wave in combination with the phenomena that accompanied the eruption (earthquakes, ashes) probably produced irreparable damages in buildings as well as in the economy and human resources of the island. Although the palace complexes of Crete were reconstructed after the disaster, they could never regain their former glory.

Nevertheless, some elements of the myth, such as the geographical location of Atlantis beyond the Strait of Gibraltar and its enormous land area make the above-mentioned identification precarious. Besides, Crete never sank in spite of the serious destruction to which it was subjected because of the volcanic eruption.

There are other theories, which attempt to explain the mystery, which covers the sinking of Atlantis. It is probable that the Egyptian priests altered some elements of the myth and attributed the destruction of a thriving civilization, such as the Minoan civilization, to the sinking of the island. Or it is also possible that Plato wanted to present to his fellow citizens an ideally organized state, which was condemned to annihilation by the gods when people ceased to obey the laws, and merged the historic memories of many different events and fabricated the myth of the lost state by drawing data out of the real event of the Santorini eruption.

Santorini and Nea and Palia Kameni after the 1867 eruption. Fouqué 1879.

Sketch of Nea Kameni

N. KAMENI
LAVA
(1707-1711)

DAPHNE LAVA
(1925-1926)

PEROULIO

MIKRI
KAMENI
(1570)

DAPHNE LAVA
(1925-1926)

FOUQUÉ LAVA
(1939-1940)

AFROESSA LAVA 1866

FOUQUÉ DAPHNE

1

2   3
o
4   5

NIKE (1940-41)

REK
LAVA
(1940)

GEORGE I
(1866-1870)

GEORGE I LAVA
(1866-1870)

1: Rek Vault (1940)

2 - 3: Smith Vaults (A&B)

4: Twin Tunnel (1940)

5: Liatsikas Vault (1950)

THE VOLCANIC ERUPTIONS

During the historic era the volcano erupted fourteen times. The eruptions were not of the same intensity and were less potent than those that created the caldera around 1650 BC.

One of these eruptions took place after a 1500-year old quietness, in 46 BC, or according to other sources in 197 AD or 194 AD and had as a result the creation of Palia Kameni.

According to Strabo, in 197 AD the lava of the new potent upheaval created the Iera island, which as the French geologist F. Fouqué maintains is the submarine dome called "Bagos" that was covered by ashes from Daphne in 1925-26.

In 19 AD, the Thea island was created, which according to F. Fouqué, is the contemporary Palia Kameni.

In 726 BC, lava from the volcano created an islet that according to the view of certain researchers after it had joined the Iera island disappeared, while others maintain that this islet must have been created to the north of Palea Kameni which it joined later.

There follows a period of volcanic calmness, which lasted approximately 850 years.

In 1570 or 1573, a new phase of upheavals began. In this stage Mikri Kameni was created.

In 1570, a submarine eruption took place outside the caldera this time on the northeast of Santorini, in a 6,5-kilometer distance from Kolumbo cape and created an islet, which was later covered by sea. Today there is a small shoal in a 19-meter depth under sea level. The eruption was accompanied by powerful earthquakes, clouds, steam and poisonous gazes, terrible blasts, volcanic ashes which were carried by the winds to Asia Minor and tidal waves which covered a big part of Santorini and hit Crete.

In 1707-1711, an islet was created between Palea and Mikri Kameni, called Nea Kameni.

1866-1870: The vaults of George I are created and on the west the Afroessa ones, which joined Nea Kameni, as well as the May islets (reefs between Palea and Nea Kameni).

1925-1926: Volcanic lava created the Daphne vault between Nea and Mikri Kameni, which covers the sea straits lying between them. Thus, the two islets were joined together.

In 1928 the Nautilus vault was created.

1939-1941: Eight new vaults were created. The Triton I and II, Ktenas, Fouqué, Smith I and II, Rek and Nike while on the George I vault (on the east of its peak) a large funnel-like cavity was created which consists of two smaller ones and was accordingly named "Twin Funnel".

In 1950 the Liatsikas vault was created on the eastern slopes of the George I vault.

**IMPORTANT EVENTS
IN THE HISTORY OF SANTORINI**

On this island, the existence of which is inextricably linked to the volcanic activity, traces of human presence are found (pottery and statuettes) already since the mid-third millenium BC (approximately 3000 BC) when the Protocycladic civilization was in its second phase (3200-2000 BC).

FROM THE PREHISTORIC ERA
UNTIL THE ROMAN PERIOD

Traces of life are present during the next period, the Mesocycladic, while there is evidence only about the first phase of the late Bronze Age as the finds of the important excavation at Akrotiri attest (See p. 42).

The inhabitants during this period must have not only been farmers but also experienced seamen. After the tremendous eruption of the volcano, that during the last years the researchers tend to place a few decades before the end of the 17th century BC, Thera, scattered and buried under thick layers of ash as it was, remained deserted at least for the two coming centuries. Evidence from the next period (pieces of Mycenean pots in the Monolithos area) indicates that the island was again inhabited not before the end of the 13th C BC.

The historian Herodotus writes that the first inhabitants after the destruction of the island were Phoenicians. According to the myth, while the Phoenician king Cadmus was searching for his sister Europe who was abducted by Zeus, disguised as a white bull, stopped in Kallisti (meaning the most beautiful, a name given to Santorini for its beauty by the Phoenicians). He left Meliambros behind to colonize it while he went on to reach Central Greece, founded Theba and brought the

Phoenician alphabet to the Greeks. Herodotus places the arrival of the
Dorians to Kallisti eight generations after Cadmus, that is around 1115
BC. The colonizer was Theras, in honour of whom the Spartans named
the island. Theras the son of Autesion, who was a Theban hero and a
Cadmus' offspring, lived in Sparta as viceroy and guardian of his orphan
nephews Procles and Eurysthenes. Upon their coming of age, he left
Sparta for reasons of status and settled in Santorini. It is certain that in
the 9th century BC, Thera was a Doric colony. Its centre was the Ancient
Thera settlement on the fortified site of Mesa Vouno (See p. 66). It constitutes together with the southeastern coasts of Greece, Crete, Melos and
Cyprus the connecting bridge between East and West. Very little is known
about life in Thera during this period (geometric). Despite the fact that
society was closed and received only a few influences from the outside world because of the adoption of the Spartan austere principals and
ideals, in the end of the 9th or the beginning of the 8th century BC, about
825 BC, Thera was the first, together with Crete and Melos, to adopt the
Phoenician alphabet. There is evidence of contact between Santorini and
Attica, Corinth, Rhodes and Ionia during the archaic period (7th and 6th
centuries BC). But generally, the conservative and austere inhabitants of
Thera preferred agricultural occupations and cattle breeding to seafaring. Even the establishment of their unique colony, Cyrene, on the northern coasts of Africa where contemporary Libya lies, seems that it was
instigated by need. As Herodotus informs us, they were obliged to set
forth this long journey after seven years of draught and following a Delphi
oracle. Already since the 6th century Thera had its own mint which
interrupted its function during the Persian Wars and was restored after
the end of the Athenian hegemony in the Aegean, that is around the
mid-4th century BC.
During the Classical Age (5th and 4th centuries BC), the Spartan men-
tality and the isolation of the inhabitants impeded Thera from playing

an important role in the region's history. In the Peloponnesian War the Therans allied themselves to the Spartans.

In 426/425 BC the island was subjugated by the Athenians and became a part of the Athenian League. When the Macedonians prevailed, it was drawn into their sphere of influence.

During the Hellenistic Age (323-146 BC), the particularly useful strategic site of Mesa Vouno, obliged the Ptolemies to use Thera as an advanced base for their war operations.

After the Roman conquest in 146 BC, the island was unimportant within the enormous territory of the Roman Empire.

FROM THE BYZANTINE TO THE MODERN AGE

In the Byzantine period, Santorini acquired a certain political and military importance. It was incorporated into the Byzantine Empire and formed part of the Aegean Sea province.

Christianity most likely reached the island in the 3rd century AD. Thus in the 4th century there was an organized community into the Diocese of Thera. The prosperity of the local Christian community during the early-Christian period is evidenced by the presence of three early-Christian basilicas. The first one was built on the site of Ancient Thera, in Mesa Vouno and was dedicated to the Archangel Michael. On its ruins the two-aisled barrel-vaulted basilica of St. Stephen was built in the 14th or 15th century (See p. 70). The second one was situated where the Byzantine church of the Virgin Mary of Piskopi Gonias lies. It was a tri-aisled domed basilica and was probably erected in the end of the 6th century or in the beginning of the 7th. The third one, finally, was built in Perissa where today the ruins of the tri-aisled basilica of St. Irene are situated.

Despite the fact that the expansion of the Arabs in North Africa and the incursions of pirates emphasized the importance of the Aegean Islands during the Byzantine Age (395-1204), the volcano and the relatively infertile soil of Thera did not favour its development. Only in the 9th and 10th centuries the island's population increased due to the developing commercial activity in the Aegean, which exploited the natural nautical capacity of the island.

In 1153 AD, we meet for the first time in the writings of the Arab geographer Edrises the island's new name: Santorini. The crusaders probably named it after the small St. Irene church (Santa Irini – Santorini). The location of the small church is debated, some maintain that it was in Perissa and others in Riva of Theresia.

After the conquest of Constantinople by the crusaders of the Fourth Crusade in 1204 and the creation of the Latin Empire of Bosporus, Dandolos grant-

View of the interior of the Panayia Piskopi Gonias church which was probably built between 1081 and 1118.

ed the Aegean Islands to this nephew Marco Sanudo. Thus the Duchy of Naxos or of the Archipelago was founded. In his turn, Marco Sanudo granted Thera together with Therasia as a barony to Iakovos Varotsis. The Orthodox bishop was exiled and a Latin one was established on the island. Then Santorini became one of the four Latin dioceses of the Duchy. During this period, the capital of the island because of the fear of incursions by pirates was located in the Skaros fort.

In 1335 the Varotsis family was expelled from the island and Thera was again annexed to the Duchy of Naxos. Under the Sanoudi hegemony, the island prospered because of the development of cotton farming.

From 1396 until 1418 Santorini was under the protection of the duke James of Crispi. In 1480 the Duke of Naxos James III Crispi gave the island as a dowry to his daughter Florence and her husband Dominic Pizani who was the son of the Duke of Crete. After James' death, his brother John III occupied Thera and annexed it again to the Duchy of Naxos. Despite the interventions of Venice which became the master of the island and of the Duchy in 1487, the Crispi family continued to rule the Duchy of Naxos for many years. During the Frankish rule, the island suffered both from the antagonism among local rulers and from pirates who preyed upon the Aegean coasts already since the Byzantine period. For these reasons the inhabitants fortified various sites and organized fortified settlements, called castellia (castles) which were situated in almost inaccessible points, far away from the sea. These castles were five: Skaros, Epanomeria, Pyrgos, Niborio and Akrotiri (See p. 76).

In 1537 the terrible pirate Naireddin Barbarossa captured Thera and handed it to the sultan. Then the Orthodox diocese of Santorini

The holy water in the yard of the Panaya Piskopi Gonias church.

One of the five kastelia of Santorini was dominant in Pyrgos, the so-called Kenouriobourgo, built since the Byzantine years.

was reestablished. Nonetheless, the Crispi family continued the nominal government of the island until 1566 when the last Crispi was removed from his office. Thera devolved definitively to the direct rule of the Turks in 1579 when the Jew Joseph Nazis to whom the Sublime Port had granted many Aegean islands and Santorini between them died. In fact the Turks never set foot on the island to which they gave the name Deimerzik that means Small Mill because of its windmills. They imposed taxes and left Franks and Greeks to resolve their problems alone as the relations between them already since the period of Frankish rule were not always harmonious. The Catholics tried hard to reinforce their presence on the island by building churches, monasteries and schools. In 1642 Jesuits missionaries were established on the island and began a systematic effort to proselytize the Orthodox community to Catholicism. At the same time the Greek Orthodox community made its own efforts to prevail by building its own churches and schools and by keeping the Greek culture and language alive. Around the end of the 17th century the number of Catholics was reduced as the class which consisted of descendents of the Latin conquerors declined. The only resource for the local nobility was trade to which first the Franks turned, followed by locals who gradually left them lagging behind. The production of the famous local wines and the intensive farming of cotton encouraged the inhabitants to create a remarkable fleet for the transportation of the island's products. Thus, Thera began to prosper. In 1780 the Prophet Elias monastery owned a boat while

in Armeni of Epanomeria and in Athinios two shipyards were in function. In the beginning of the 19th century seafaring continues to thrive. The economic autonomy of the island is preserved and its prosperity is reflected on the old mansions, which are still to be seen on the villages of Santorini. In 1821 Thera took part in the Independence War. Its fleet was the third after the fleets of Hydra and Spetses while the Prophet Elias monastery contributed 1,640 piastres for the needs of the struggle. Upon the creation of the Greek state in 1832 Santorini was united with the rest of Greece. Around 1850, Santorini increased its trade and became the first commercial power among the Aegean Islands. Most of its wine production was sold in Russia in exchange for cereals. The islanders used a certain quantity of cereals for consumption on the island and the rest of it was sold in France, Italy and England. A part of the ash, which was quarried locally, was exported to Austria and the rest of it was given to the Greek State for the construction of hydraulic works and harbours.

After 1910 the vessels used for maritime transport changed. The inability of the local ship-owners to adjust to the new conditions signaled the beginning of a long decay for the island, which compounded with the 1956 earthquakes when entire sections of the settlements were destroyed. Today, the Santorini of those days looks very distant. The pictures of disaster and abandonment gave their place to the contemporary reality, which has transformed the island into one of the most popular tourist resorts of the Aegean.

AKROTIRI,
THE PREHISTORIC TOWN

Until the end of the 19th century, our knowledge about the prehistoric civilizations of the Aegean was limited. The excavations of Knossos in Crete by Evans and the excavations of Troy, Mycenae and Tirynth by Schliemann accompanied the first decade of the 20th century. In 1939 Professor Spiros Marinatos formulated a theory according to which the decay of the Minoan civilization was due to the tremendous eruption of the Santorini volcano (which was then estimated at around 1500 BC). The violent destruction of a Minoan villa that he excavated in Amnisos (the harbour of Knossos) in combination with the discovery of pumice and volcanic materials on the basement of another building which was situated near the sea, led him to the conclusion that the volcanic eruption produced huge tidal waves that reached the coasts of Crete and destroyed the splendid Minoan palace. His will to verify this theory led him to initiate excavations in Thera in 1967.

THE BACKGROUND OF THE EXCAVATIONS

East side of Complex D. The door and window of room 2, where the famous mural of the Spring was found, are distinguished.

Already since 1860 relics of prehistoric facilities were found in a quarry in Therasia. Buried under thick layers of volcanic ash, they were brought to light on the occasion of quarrying ashes destined for the construction of the Suez Canal. The first excavation at the Therasia quarry took place in 1866. In 1867 the French geologist F. Fouqué who was in Thera in order to study the eruptions of the volcano continued the excavations. In 1870 two members of the French Archaeological School, H. Mamet and H. Gorceix, with the encouragement of their compatriot

F. Fouqué undertook a small scale excavation of the Therasia quarry and studied prehistoric findings in the major Akrotiri area. In 1895 simultaneously to the excavations undertaken by the German baron H. v. Gaertringen in Mesa Vouno, which had as a result the discovery of the Ancient Thera relics, a team of his colleagues again searched the Akrotiri area and uncovered important prehistoric relics. When Spiros Marinatos began his effort to locate the prehistoric town of Santorini, he preferred to excavate Akrotiri to all the other excavated sites such as Ballos, Archangelos, and Therasia on which relics had been found. It was the easiest accessible of all the other sites; there were still visible traces of shells, pots etc. on the surface; the most important architectural relics were located here by the French researchers and finally its geographic location, which was near the sea and opposite Crete, favoured the development of a large prehistoric settlement. Despite the fact that the conclusions of the last three archaeological excavations tend to refute the Marinatos' theory, as the dating of pottery samples from Akrotiri and Crete proves that the decay of the Minoan civilization began several years after the eruption of the volcano and was probably the result of other factors (perhaps because of the descent of Achaeans), these excavations brought to light a very important and perfectly preserved prehistoric town which was a prominent centre of the Aegean when it thrived during the first half of the second millenium BC. The ruins of the prehistoric town that we can see today belong to first period of the Late Bronze Age, the Late Minoan referring to Crete, and the Late Cycladic referring to the Cyclades Islands. In the same area relics of pottery of the Mid-Cycladic Age were found while there are indications that the Mid-Cycladic buildings of the settlement contained frescoes. The French geologist Fouqué called the settlement Pompey of the Aegean. The thick volcanic banking ups which covered its ruins preserved the buildings and their chattels intact. These remains of human activity give the impression that the Minoan civ-

This Minoan rhyton decorated with rosettes and mouldings was imported from Crete and found in Akrotiri.

From Akrotiri the painted offering table made of lime mortar and decorated with dolphins.

Athens, National Archaeological Museum.

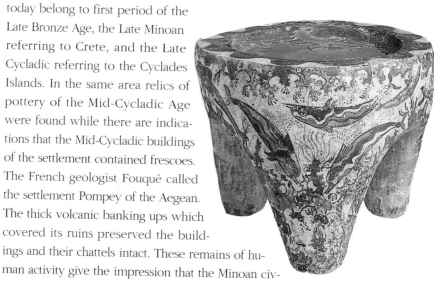

ilization had a substantial impact on the life of this town, which nonetheless managed to preserve its own cultural identity. The limits and area of the settlement are not known, as the excavations are not yet completed. According to professor Doumas the currently excavated area, which covers a surface of 10,000 m², constitutes the 1/30 of the total surface that was supposedly occupied by the prehistoric town.

URBANISM AND ARCHITECTURE
OF THE PREHISTORIC TOWN

As you enter into the excavation site you can see two-storeyed buildings or even three-storeyed ones, which sometimes are connected to each other and create large complexes or stand alone, surrounded by narrow stone-paved roads that in some places broaden and create small squares (such as the Triangular square in front of the West House). They contain many rooms and are built with small asymmetric stones, which abounded in the area while the walls are supported by wooden constructions so as to resist the earthquakes. Hewn stones are used to mark the level of each floor in multi-storeyed buildings or cover the entire façade of greater buildings, which are called Xestes (Hewn).

Under the stone-pavement of the roads there are sewers which served the drainage system while the unclean waters reached the system through ceramic tubes which were incorporated into the buildings' walls. Almost every house contained a sanitary discharge, which was connected to the central sewing system.

The buildings have no yards and their entrances stand directly on the roads and squares while their configuration is original. They are usually doors of big dimensions framed by hewn stones. Next to the door there is often a window.

The settlement's buildings are divided into public constructions and private homes. The latter are smaller and their arrangement seems to be dictated by their use.

It seems that every house ensured autarky to its tenants. On the basement lie the auxiliary rooms, which served the everyday basic needs of the household such as the storage of food, grinding of crops and cooking. The rooms, which lie on the upper floors, had frescoes on the walls and functioned as the main house. The basement rooms had no murals. Those that functioned as storerooms had small windows for the necessary ventilation, humidity, light and temperature in order to preserve food. When the basement was used as a work-shop, there was a big window next to the door. Moreover, the installation of a mill for the grinding of grain

The staircase on the northern entrance of Complex D which was leading to the first floor.

or other crops was indispensable in almost every household.

The public buildings are impressive as to their size and have a well-structured masonry. Besides the upper floor rooms, the ground floor walls are often frescoed as it happens in the Xesti 3 basement, the so-called "Lustral Basin" which must have been a cult site.

In the Akrotiri edifices the upper floor rooms communicated with the basement through an interior stone- and sometimes wooden staircase. They were spacious and were lit abundantly by big windows. It seems that the loom was a necessary piece of furniture for the upper floor rooms of private houses. The buildings' floors were usually made of rammed earth and sometimes were paved with slate plaques, iridescent splinters from sea-shells or small pebbles that create a mosaic-like effect. The roofs were horizontal and earthen. It is worth noticing that even today there are houses with earthen roofs in Greek islands, which offer to their tenants coolness during the summer and warmth during the winter. Finally, both the outside and inside walls of every edifice were coated. The coat was a fine mortar made of lime, often coloured (ruddy, yellow, and whitish). The murals, which as we have seen decorated chiefly the upper floors, were usually painted over the white coat.

LIFE IN THE PREHISTORIC TOWN

As the many finds from the excavations reveal, life in Akrotiri was rich, comfortable and sophisticated and reminds us of life in the Minoan palace. Although there are no written documents to provide information about the Akrotiri economic structure and social stratification, it can be deduced that a part of its richness originated in trade and shipping. The imported goods and murals attest to the relations with Crete and

Above:
The entrance to room 2 of complex D -depicted here- was effected through the yard or through another room while it had double walls in three of its sides.

Below:
Earthenware jars orderly placed next to each other brought to light by excavations.

continental Greece, Egypt and generally with the Eastern Mediterranean peoples. Although there is no evidence that Thera exported goods to other locations, it is almost certain that local boats were involved in trading activities between Crete, Egypt, Syria and Palestine.

The island's climate during that period must have been less dry than the current one and its soil arable. Its fauna consisted of hares and red deer.

Besides trade, agriculture, cattle rearing and fishing seem to be the basic occupations of the Akrotiri inhabitants, which was apparently a centre of a very intense activity.

The substantial quantities of carbonized fruits found inside earthenware jars, the mills' facilities and the decorated with representations of grapes and barley ear-corns pots inform us that barley, legumes (split peas), peas and vines were the principle crops on the island. Other products include flour, figs and sesame.

STONE-HEWING AND MICRO-CRAFTSMANSHIP

A host of stone implements and vessels (hammers, anvils, smoothers and graters) made of basalt, a very hard material, which abounds on the island, is found in Santorini. A small number of vessels such as basins, compasses, oil-lamps and cups made of rarer stones (marble, ofeitis, talc etc.) which were not found on the island were apparently imported.

Information about the miniature art of the period is offered by murals. Golden earrings, bracelets and necklaces made of beads are the usual feminine jewelry. It seems that the inhabitants took with them all precious objects before the tremendous volcanic eruption and therefore nothing is found in excavations. On the contrary, objects made of bronze such as frying-pans, large baking-pans, pots, single-handled vessels, amphorae as well as implements such as knives, sickles and saws which are typical samples of the Akrotiri copper works were found.

The olive-tree was most likely known long before the volcanic eruption. The women of the island were occupied in the collection of crocus as the fresco of the Female Crocus Gatherers informs us as well as in weaving and textile- and fibre dying. Among the town's ruins amphorae have been found which were specially made for the transport of oil; earthenware jars used to keep the wine and conic horn-like jars used to measure and empty liquids into smaller pots.

The Akrotiri inhabitants bred sheep, pigs and cattle while such frescoes as those depicting fishermen as well as other findings (seashells, fish relics etc) testify to their occupation also in fishing. The presence of large amounts of murexes, namely of the shell, which produces the deep purple dye-stuff, indicate their use for the production of the rhodopsin colour. Thousands of local pots, vessels and implements serve as evidence of the existence of work-shops with specialized artisans while a great part of the island's working force was occupied in the construction and decoration of houses.

The riches, which probably were the fruit of shipping activities, seem

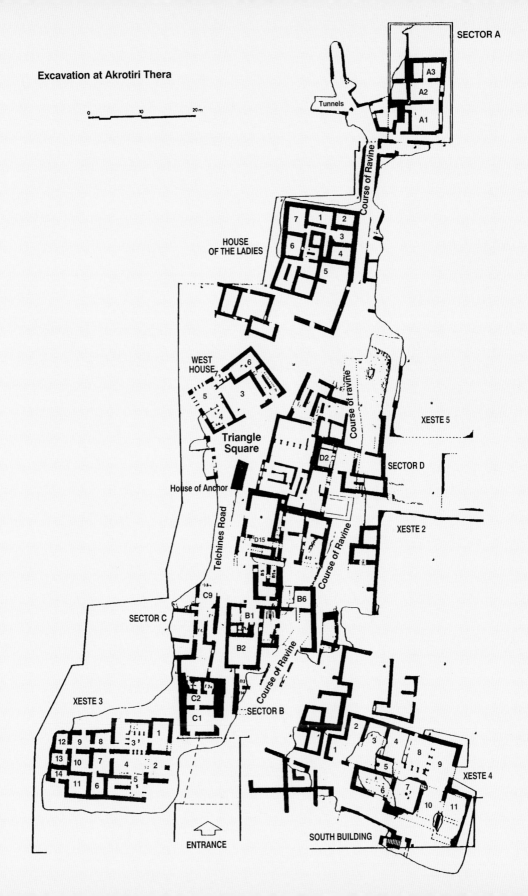

Excavation at Akrotiri Thera

SECTOR A

A3
A2
A1

Tunnels

Course of Ravine

HOUSE
OF THE LADIES

7 1 2
6   3
      4
   5

WEST
HOUSE

6
5 3
4

Triangle
Square

House of Anchor

Course of ravine

XESTE 5

D2

SECTOR D

XESTE 2

Telchines Road

D15

Course of Ravine

C9

B6

SECTOR C

B1

B5

B2

Course of Ravine

XESTE 3

C2

C1

SECTOR B

12 9 8   1
13 10 7 3 4 2
14 11 6   5

2
1 3 4
5 8
6 7 9

XESTE 4

10 11

ENTRANCE

SOUTH BUILDING

0   10   20 m

The produce of the prehistoric town was stored in big earthenware jars which are found among the ruins.

to be divided among more than one of the society members. This fact is demonstrated by the presence of big, spacious houses and the extensive use of frescoes. Moreover, the urban planning and architecture of Akrotiri, as they appear today, attest to the assumption that power was not the domain of a sole person. Perhaps, owing to this reason the up to now realized excavations did not bring to light traces of a central power. On the contrary, they indicate the presence and organization of special services, which took care of the needs of the entire social structure (e.g. service of maintenance of the sewage system).

Akrotiri was a prosperous society that in spite of the Minoan influences, to which it was subjected, remained politically, socially, religiously and artistically autonomous.

The numerous peculiarities and the independence that the researchers distinguish in architecture, pottery, pottery decoration and art are elements which support this view.

Moreover, the Minoan presence on the island is traced mainly during the Late Minoan Age while the Cycladic elements existed at least since the mid-third millenium BC and continued their evolution approximately until the end of the 17th century BC.

The end of this prosperous society was brought about by the volcanic eruption, the exact date of which is still debated. It seems that powerful earth tremors preceded the eruption and drove the inhabitants to abandon their ruined houses. It is probable that a few persons who belonged to the groups that undertook the repair of the destroyed buildings remained on the island. But they soon left the island as well. The absence of human skeletons and precious objects in the excavations leads researchers to the conclusion that inhabitants had enough time to get their things together and abandon their city before the disaster. Although the time that elapsed between the first seism and the awakening of the volcano is unknown, some data indicates that at least a year had intervened when the first ashes from the eruption began to fling.

THE AKROTIRI PAINTING

Undoubtedly the most developed of all arts in Akrotiri was painting. Such a conclusion becomes evident from the impressive murals brought to light. These fine frescoes in addition to their artistic value give precious information about nature and life in the prehistoric town.

In the private houses they decorate the rooms' walls that served the social needs of the owners while in the public buildings, the spaces used for certain ceremonies. They cover various surfaces, both in shape and dimensions. They decorate door and window jambs, small surfaces on walls between two openings, window planks, zones created by the openings of cupboards or windows and finally big wall surfaces. Often, a composition is developed not only on one but also on more walls of the same room or even of adjacent rooms, a typical element of the Cycladic painting.

The due to be painted surface was divided into three zones, the lower zone, which

Detail from the Micrography of the Procession of Ships. Precious information about the town of Akrotiri is offered by this fine mural which has a narrative character.

Athens, National Archaeological Museum.

*The mural of the
Fisherman who
holds two strings of
fish decorated
room 5 of the
Western House.*

*Athens, National
Archaeological
Museum.*

was the base of the main composition, the middle one, on which the principal theme was developed and finally the upper one which was covered either by decorative motives or micrographic friezes.

The colours mostly used were red, black, yellow, azure and white. Azure was used to depict water, the plumage of birds, fishes, dolphins, apes, the shaved heads of young men and women and some plants such as lilies, reeds, papyruses, ivies and palm-trees. The red colour was used to represent men's complexion, while white for women's. As for ochre it was used for the depiction of lions' fur and the light green of plants such as the myrtle and osier.

The local artist classifies the human figures he paints according to their age. Thus mature men and women are represented with rich black hair, a double chin and a well-defined belly. On the contrary, younger figures have short curly hair. As for children, boys appeared nude and girls dressed. They both have a blue head, which means that their hair is either cut short or shaved.

In spite of certain Minoan influences, the Thera murals are distinguished for their independence from Cretan art conventionalities, the freedom in design, composition and movements which indicate an influence on themes and style explained by contacts between Thera and the Eastern Mediterranean and chiefly Egypt.

The fresco of the so-called **Young Priestess** –taken from the rich in murals West House- depicts a young woman dressed with a long, heavy, probably woolen tunic holding an incensory with burning coals and moving towards room 5. This particular fresco united rooms 4 and 5 of the first floor of the West House. The eastern edge of the northern wall and the southern edge of the western wall of room 5 of the same house were decorated with two fine frescoes depicting **Fishermen** each one of whom holds a bunch of fishes.

On the upper zone of the four walls of room 5 in the West House –namely on the oblong surface which stretched above doors and windows- the **Micrographic Frieze** was developed, an important monument of Aegean art.

According to the conclusions of researchers the Frieze 'narrates' in a particularly expressive manner the long journey of a fleet during which it visited various cities and regions.

On the part of the frieze that occupied the northern wall the artist depicts, in a manner demonstrating great quality and sensibility, scenes in three levels (the **Shipwreck** micrography). On the first level we see a rocky coast and three nude men in the water who look drowned. The shields beside them as well as the position of the boat's bow reinforce the view that we are looking at a representation of a naval battle whose victims were the three dead fighters. On the second level, the coast is represented fortified with a surrounding wall (Town II), built on the estuary of a river, which was visited by the fleet while a group of fighters walks in a single file holding rectangular shields, long pikes and swords and wearing casques made of boar tusk which constituted the typical Aegean armament of the period. On the third –upper- level, two shepherds try to pen in their flock, a few men stand in front of a well, perhaps chatting, while two women leave the scene after having filled up their pitchers.

On the eastern part of the frieze scenes from the life of wild animals beside the river are depicted (Micrography of the **River** or of the **Subtropical Landscape**) while the representation of a town and a boat in the beginning of the eastern section led researchers to believe

TECHNIQUE

As for the technique, the local artist used both frescoes and xerography. The surfaces due to be painted were covered with a mixture of mud and straw and then coated with successive layers of coat.

His themes varied: He painted landscapes, nature scenes, inanimate objects, plants, animals and people or even a real event. Some murals have purely decorative motives while others depict a religious theme. All of them are marked by an intense naturalism.

Some of the frescoes that decorated in the past the prehistoric town buildings are restored, and the restoration of the remaining ones is undertaken by professor Christos Doumas who continues the work of Spiros Marinatos.

that it was a coastal town (Town III) built on a river estuary and probably visited by the fleet.

The hand of the unknown Theran artist brilliantly depicts the fauna and flora of the hinterland of the region visited by the fleet. A wild duck flies, a kid runs on one riverside while on the other a wild cat rushes at the wild ducks sitting there. The existence on the murals of landscapes that do not resemble the immediate environment of the Theran artists indicates journeys to other lands. This explains the familiarity of local artists with animals that live elsewhere, such as antelopes, apes, lions, deer etc. The best-preserved segment of the Frieze is the northern one, the Micrography of the **Procession of Ships** on which sailing boats are depicted departing from a town (Town IV) and reaching another (Town V) which looks like Akrotiri. The architecture of the towns depicted on the fresco is similar to that of the excavation, multi-storeyed buildings constructed with hewn stones on different levels. The decking of the flagship and the numerous dolphins, which play beside the ships, led the archaeologists to the conclusion that its passengers are warriors. The inhabitants of both cities are outside their houses and those represented on the left-hand side bid farewell while those on the right-hand side welcome the warriors. It is not unlikely that the scene represents a real event. This fresco is a unique source of information about life in the Aegean during the last decades of the 17th century BC. Besides the information about archi-

It seems that the Micrography of the Procession of Ships, which covered the upper part of the four walls of room 5 of the Western House, is a segment of the Micrographic Frieze. Sailing boats departing from a city and arriving in another are depicted there.

Athens, National Archaeological Museum.

tecture, costumes, flora and fauna, it is the first time that we have such a detailed representation of prehistoric vessels. We can draw valuable data about naval architecture and operation of boats during the above-mentioned period. The skill of the Theran artist is admirable. A very impressive element is the concept of space and the rendering of the background. Only two parts are preserved from the fresco of **Women** or **Ladies**, from room 1 of the second floor of the House of Women. Two female figures (one of which is bare-breasted) are represented almost in natural size with loose black hair wearing rich costumes and jewelry. Azure rhombuses with concave sides which join each other through dotted red lines cover the upper zone of the wall.

The **Pangration** or according to another view **Papyruses** fresco also decorated the same room in the House of Women, with the representation of blooming flowers springing up from the soil.

Three out of the four walls of room 2 on the ground floor of Complex D are covered by the fine mural of the **Lilies** or of **Spring**. Lilies bloom in a rocky landscape while swallows are flirting in the air. The colours are almost impressionist and the stalks of the triple lilies are rendered so naturally by the artist so as to give the impression that there is a spring-breeze blowing. The rocks which are either yellow, green (they are painted with a deep grey colour) or red take strange shapes and remind of volcanic areas. Thus the artist probably represented a Santorini landscape as it was before the eruption.

The famous mural of the Lilies or Spring covered three out four walls of room 2. Lilies are sprouting from the rocks while the swallows that fly around them forebode the coming of spring. The colours are almost impressionist and the stems of the lilies are depicted with such a naturalistic way that they give the impression of a sway under the spring breeze.

Athens, National Archaeological Museum. →

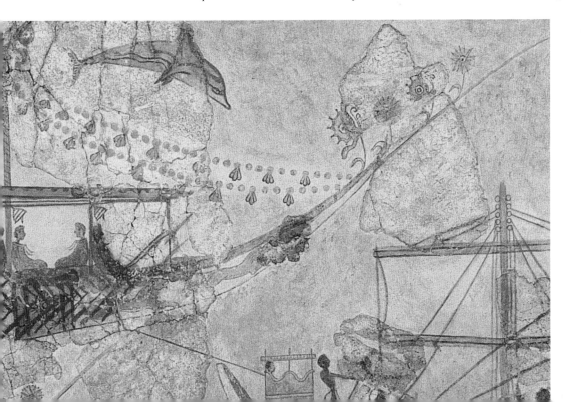

The fresco of the two young **Boxers** who wear boxing gloves and look as if they are fighting covered the southern wall of room 1, on the upper floor of building B.

The three remaining walls (western, northern and eastern) of the same room were decorated with the representation of the **Antelopes** the figures of which are painted with such simplicity so as to give a perfectly convincing result. The branch that surrounds the picture is a sample of the decorative patterns, which match the purely representative scenes in variety and perfection.

The fresco of the **Monkeys** originates in room 6 of the upper floor of the above-mentioned building. Notwithstanding its incomplete state, it is characterized by vividness and movement. An unknown cause seems to drive the apes to climb hastily on the rocks.

Below: The mural of the Antelopes painted with accuracy and full of movement.

Right: The mural of the two young Boxers who wear boxing gloves and look as if they are fighting.

Athens, National Archaeological Museum.

POTTERY

The excavations in Akrotiri brought to light in addition to frescoes rich samples of prehistoric pottery. Pots of approximately fifty different shapes were found. A lot of them were locally produced while others were imported.

The imported ones come mostly from Crete and some from continental Greece. They are less numerous than the local ones but of a superior quality. The clay they are made of is reddish, quite pure and relatively well baked.

The Cretan pots present a greater variety in decoration in comparison to the continental ones. The arrangement of themes into zones, the use of the upper part of the pot as a decorative surface, a preference for abstract lineal motives (spirals, bands, rosettes etc.) are some of the basic traits of Minoan pottery which appear also on the Minoan pots of Akrotiri. The motives –abstract, lineal and flora themes- were painted with a black shinning colour on the reddish surface of the pot. From the flora there was a special preference shown by the artists for the depiction of branches of myrtle, crocus, ivy, caper; on the contrary there is a total absence of fauna themes. Perhaps, for practical reasons related to their easy transportation, these pots were mostly small.

The local pots are also found in bigger sizes and present an infinite variety of shapes and decorative motives. Thousands of conic little cups, dozens of tripod pots, amphorae, earthenware jars, baths, various single-handled vessels used for the transfusion of liquids, strainers, flower-pots, vases etc. were used as everyday as well as luxury vessels. The latter are small and very refined both in form and decoration. Among this host of vessels which are basically local imitations of Minoan originals, some vessels which are purely Cycladic are also included (breast-shaped vessels, cylindrical flowerpots, strainers), a proof that local production continued to be alive de-

Pitcher from Akrotiri decorated with birds.

Athens, National Archaeological Museum.

spite intense Minoan influences. The clay used for local pots was whitish and not always well baked. Dark motives were usually painted on a light-coloured surface. The basic characteristics of local pottery and at the same time its distinction from the Minoan one are the almost equal use of representative and abstract themes and the free decoration of the entire pot surface and not only of zones.

THE PREHISTORIC TOWN TODAY

Our visit to the town of Akrotiri, which most likely stretched from north to south, will start from its southern part. The undertaken research has uncovered a road of the prehistoric settlement together with the buildings erected on both sides. This road, which runs across the town from north to south and which apparently led to the harbour, was called by the archaeologists, road of Telchines.

Pitcher from Akrotiri decorated with barley ears.

Athens, National Archaeological Museum.

The first building we meet on our left-hand side as we enter the excavation site has been called **Xesti 3.** It is a three-storeyed building, at least as far as its western side is concerned, with approximately fourteen rooms on the ground- and first floor. Its façade was coated with hewn stones while two stair-wells, the main one at the entrance and the secondary one in the interior, led to the first floor. There was a small courtyard in front of its entrance and beside the front door a built bench. Rooms 2, 3 and 4 of the first floor and 2, 3, 4 and 7 of the ground floor communicated through multiple doors creating a big united hall.

On the northeastern corner of the ground floor there was a "Lustral Basin" (3a) which seems to be a cult site. Its construction follows the Minoan pattern. Its bottom lies lower from the surface level of the rest of the ground floor while on its northern and eastern walls a fresco was developed (the Female Worshippers fresco), the theme of which seems to have a sacred character. On the eastern wall, an edifice is depicted which most likely represents an altar or a sanctuary while on the northern wall three elegant female figures that wear rich Minoan costumes and ornate jewelry head towards the altar. The first one is holding a necklace of beads from mineral crystals and walks to the sanctuary, the second one is sitting on the floor and is bending slightly while she is touching with her hand the wounded tow of her foot, and the third one, covered by a transparent veil, is stretching her arms forward and is turning her head backwards. According to the researchers this mural depicts an initiation scene.

The large dimensions of the building, its arrangement, the existence of the so-called "Lustral Basin", the lack of utensils and the frescoes which decorate most of the walls even those of the ground floor led the researchers to believe that it was a public building.

Among the many murals found in Xesti 3 are the Female Crocus Gatherers (room 3a of the first floor), the Female Worshippers ("Lustral Basin"), the Nude Boys (room 3b of the ground floor) and the fresco with the ornamental motives which decorated the walls of room 9 of the second floor.

To the east of Xesti 3, to our left-hand side, another building probably public has been unearthed which is called Xesti 4. It is a particularly big building with three floors and an impressive façade. Its walls are coated with hewn stones (xestes) while murals decorate its interior. After entering the **road of Telchines** (the excavated road), the next building we meet on its western side and which is partly studied is the **complex C.** It is an edifice with at least two floors only some rooms of which lying along the road are uncovered. The building must have sustained extensive damage during the earthquakes that preceded the eruption and the parties that cleaned the ruins of the town after the seism must have roughly repaired it.

On the east of the road of Telchines rises **building B**, a relatively big edifice, which scientists, based on the kind of objects found

THE WEST HOUSE

The West House is a typical small rich house. From its entrance, which lies on the northeastern corner of the square, a staircase leads to the first and second floors of the building, while a secondary staircase situated about the middle of the northern side connects the ground floor with the first floor.

The most important apartments of the house were situated on the western wing of the first floor, which was richly frescoed. A door on the northwestern corner of the adjoining room 3 led to this wing, which was divided into three smaller spaces by thin walls. On the southwestern corner of the non-frescoed room 4a water-closet facilities are found. Beside it and before room 5, lies space 4, which was a small independent room and in front of spaces 4 and 4a the oblong space 4b is situated. Besides the western wing and room 3, this floor had two more rooms, a corridor (7) on the northern side and next to it a cabinet and room 6 which contained many ceramic vessels. Room 3 had a big window giving at the square, probably a weaving room.

From the western wing, spaces 4 and 4b were decorated with the frescoes of Ikrioi while the walls of room 5 were decorated with the representations of two Fishermen, the so-called Young Priestess and the Micrographic Frieze.

The halls of the ground floor were used as workshops for storing, cooking as well as for other auxiliary activities.

there, classified into the private houses. The damage caused by the torrent that passed from it was serious enough so as to obstruct the localization of the front door as well as of the passages of communication between its halls with the exception of a secondary interior staircase.

In the ground-floor room 1 of this two-storeyed edifice, earthenware-jars are found placed in specially made niches. Beside them lie scattered conic single-handled vessels, which were probably used for the emptying of liquids. In the ground-floor room 2, many cooking-pots and conic cups were located. The walls of room 1, on the upper floor were decorated with the murals of the Children Boxers and of Antelopes while room 6 on the same floor was decorated with the fresco of the Monkeys.

Continuing northwards, we reach the **Miller's Square**, which borders on building B and complex D. The Square owes its name to a flour mill which lies in room 15 of building D.

The **complex D** was a huge building complex two- or three-storeyed which had sustained various annexes that gave to the building its final form. It has four successive doors, which correspond to the four points of the compass –the western one was protected by a pylon-, and which also correspond to the architectural stages of the edifice.

The Square of the Triangle. To its left-hand side the two-storeyed West House and to its right-hand side Complex D.

About fourteen rooms of this complex are localized at present. Room 2 of the ground floor –which belonged to the eastern building of the complex- was decorated with the fresco of Spring or of Lilies. In the same room traces of a small bed were found, a copy of which is currently exhibited in the Archaeological Museum of Athens, the traces of a stool, many pots of daily use, copper utensils and implements.

The fact that the space covered by the ground floor was frescoed –on the contrary private homes were not frescoed- as well as the unearthing of two double stone horns in front of the eastern façade of the building led the researchers to the conclusion that the site initially had a religious character but later ceased to function as such and was used as shelter for implements and utensils.

Those passing through the pylon were found on the **Square of the Triangle**, which is bigger than the Miller's Square and borders on complex D (on the southeast), the West House (on the north) and the House of the Anchor (on the southwest).

Past the West House and the northern entrance of complex D, the road of Telchines is destroyed by the torrent.

The next building we meet to our left-hand side as we continue northwards is the **House of Women**. It was a three-storeyed house, at least on the western wing, owing its name to the frescoes of Ladies or Women found in room 1 of the second floor. The finds lead to the conclusion that it was a rich private house with about ten rooms in each floor, two stair-wells, the principal one in front of the door on the southwestern side of the building and the secondary almost at its centre. On the northern side of the auxiliary staircase, there was a light well, an element found in the palatial architecture of Crete. The light well is the only one uncovered in Akrotiri at present. The southern wing of the second floor consisted of a series of rooms. A small wall separates Room 1, which was the middle one, in two sections, the eastern and western ones. Three walls –southern, western and northern- of the western section of the room were decorated with the fresco of Lilies (they are the white lilies with the heady perfume known as "sea lily") or Papyruses, while two walls –northern and southern- and probably the third one as well –eastern- of the eastern section were adorned with the Women mural.

In the building, ceramic arks were localized on the first floor and many utensils such as conic single-handled-, breast-shaped vessels and triton shells on the ground-floor room 7.

Room 1 of the second floor of the House of Women was decorated by the mural of Pangration or Papyruses.

Athens, National Archaeological Museum.

ANCIENT THERA,
THE TOWN OF THE HISTORIC ERA

As we have already seen, after the volcanic eruption of Strongyli (Thera) during the first half of the second millenium BC and the sinking of a great part of the island, Santorini remained uninhabited for many years. The next important period for the history of Santorini was closely linked to the town, the ruins of which were brought to light by the excavations that Baron Hiller von Gaertringen began in 1896.

It is the settlement of Ancient Thera in Mesa Vouno, which was the capital of the island in the historic years, founded by Doric tribes from Sparta who came to the island around 1115 BC. The Lacedaemonians chose the lime rock of Mesa Vouno both for the natural fortification of the site, its inaccessibility and steep slopes as well as for its geographic location that ensured control over southeastern Aegean. From that moment and until the expansion of Christianity, the town of Mesa Vouno, which was to be the only urban centre on the island, played an important part in the history of Thera and of the entire Aegean Sea. Before the 6th century BC, it constitutes a necessary link in the relations of Cyclades with Crete, while during the 6th century BC it will be used as an intermediate stop for the communication of Corinth and Attica with Rhodes and Ionia. A treasure of 760 silver coins found in Thera in 1821 attests to these relations. Nevertheless, nothing could change local social structure and cultural life, which remained faithful to Doric models.

Ancient Thera, built on the relatively level ridge of the mountain, is adapted to the shape and dimensions of the surface. The town's length is approximately 800 meters, and its width barely reaches 150 meters.

To the south of Kamari beach rises the lime rock of Mesa Vouno where the Lacedaemonian settlers who arrived in Santorini around 1115 BC founded their capital, Ancient Thera. From Kamari a steep winding road leads to the ruins of the town which are situated on the summit of the mountain.

The picture we have about the town of Ancient Thera is not complete as the excavations of H. v. Gaertingen were limited mainly to the sites containing public buildings. Thus, the ruins we see today belong mainly to the Hellenistic Age. Nonetheless, the limitations imposed by the natural environment led researchers to believe that the town must have had the same urban planning in every stage of its history. Namely, houses and public buildings were built on the ridge of the mountain while the cemeteries lay in Sellada, on the point that Mesa Vouno joins Prophet Elias.

It seems that the beaches of Kamari and Perissa, on the north and south of Mesa Vouno, were used as berths for local boats. Two roads connected the town with its harbours. The same roads passed through the Sellada cemeteries on the top of which they joined and led to the town.

The road network of Ancient Thera consisted of a central road which is also currently used by visitors and some smaller ones which intersected it and led to the theatre, squares, arcades, sanctuaries as well as to public and private buildings. These alleys were always stone-paved and sometimes gradient due to the sloping ground. The result was that the town as a whole had an amphitheatrical character. Covered channels, which served as a sewage system, crossed the town.

As for the burial customs of the inhabitants, information is drawn from the extensive cemeteries of the Geometric Period which lie the first one on the southwestern slope of Sellada and the second one under the steep rocks of Mesa Vouno. It seems that they were systematically used until

ARTS IN ANCIENT THERA

The samples of ceramic art of the geometric period found in Ancient Thera demonstrate the performance of the inhabitants in the artistic sector.

The earliest decorated vessels in Thera are meso-geometric cups with two horizontal handles; the lineal motives were painted directly on the clay. The jugs and amphorae (vessels used for the storage of ashes) are the most important vessels of the late-geometric years and were usually made in relatively big sizes in order to contain the burial gifts as well.

The geometric vessels are both the most ancient samples of art found in Ancient Thera and the only ones that can be attributed with certainty to local artisans. From the 6th century BC onwards, imported vessels poured into Thera. The first place was occupied by the coveted Attic vessels (black-shaped ceramics) while vessels from the pottery workshops of Rhodes, Corinth and Ionia were also present, indicating thus the places with which Thera was in contact during that period.

Moreover, in Santorini some monumental works of archaic sculpture were found. Two Couros statues dating from the 7th century BC are exhibited in the Archaeological Museum of Thera and another one from the beginning of the 6th century BC, which is known as Apollo of Thera, is now in the National Archaeological Museum of Athens. Initially these statues must have been standing on tombs belonging to illustrious members of local society in the archaic cemetery of Sellada. Their height was over 2 meters and they were made of roughly granulated island marble. They all were works of art made in Naxos.

the mid-seventh century BC, although some newer tombs of the Hellenistic and Roman periods were also located. The Therans used to burn the dead and keep their ashes together with the burial gifts into specially made vessels, which were placed inside family tombs.

The cemetery of the 6th, 5th and 4th centuries BC is stretched on the northeastern slope of Sellada. The older tombs lie generally higher than the newer ones. Podiums made of hewn marble were built on the tomb and on them, they used to place small cubic stones with the name of the deceased. During that period the inhabitants of Thera either cremated or buried the entire body of their dead. The famous Attic vessels, which are currently exhibited in the Fira Archaeological Museum, were found here.

The Ancient Thera theatre built in the 3rd century BC was one of the most important public edifices of the town of the historic era.

ANCIENT THERA TODAY

The entrance into the archaeological site of Ancient Thera is situated on the northwest and the visitor follows a southeastern direction.

Besides the edifices dating from the Archaic, Hellenistic and Roman Years we will also see the ruins of three churches. On the left-hand side of the entrance lie the remains of one of them, which belong to an early-Christian basilica of the 4th or 5th century AD, dedicated to Archangel Michael. Later, on its ruins, the St. Stephen basilica was built.

The most important, most sacred and ancient site in Ancient Thera was the great square of Gymnopaediae, which lies on the most southeasterly edge of the town. It was formed with the assistance of powerful banking-up walls, dating from the 6th century BC. On this square, the gymnopaediae were celebrated in honour of the Doric Apollo Carneios. Namely, nude boys danced and sang paeans in honour of Apollo. The admiration of the spectators for the young dancers is brilliantly stamped on the numerous erotic inscriptions carved on the rocks which in addition inform us that the feasts were celebrated here at least since the 7th century BC.

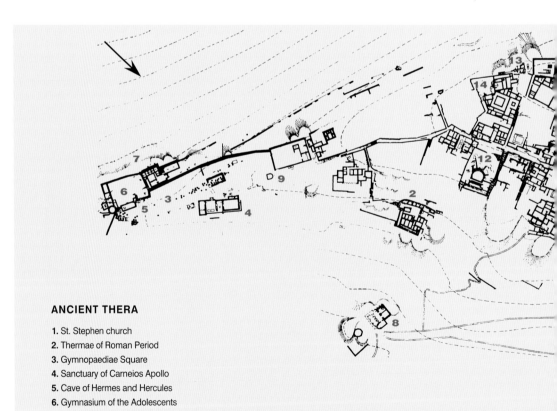

ANCIENT THERA

1. St. Stephen church
2. Thermae of Roman Period
3. Gymnopaediae Square
4. Sanctuary of Carneios Apollo
5. Cave of Hermes and Hercules
6. Gymnasium of the Adolescents
7. Roman Baths
8. Annunciation War Memorial-Church
9. Agora
10. Royal Arcade
11. Temple of Dionysus
12. Theatre
13. Temple of Anoubis, Serapes, Isis
14. Temple of Pytios Apollo
15. Shrine of Artemidorus
16. Headquarters
17. Gymnasium of the Guard

Gymnopaediae was one of the main events of the greatest festival for Thera, which it had in common with all Dorians. The festival was transplanted from Sparta and took place in mid-Carneios (namely, August or September) with the full moon. The Gymnopaediae square bordered on the **Sanctuary of Carneios Apollo** to the north, which is partly built on an artificial mound and dates from the 6th century BC. A section of the temple is hewn on the rock and the rest is built on the mound. It has no outside colonnade, and consists of the vestibule and the main temple.

Near the Gymnopaediae Square lies the opening of a small cave which was dedicated to the cult of Hermes and Hercules. Beside this den **the Gymnasium of Adolescents**, a second-century BC edifice and the **Roman Baths** are situated while about 100 meters to the northeast of the Carneios Apollo sanctuary lies the **Annunciation** tiny war memorial-church. It is one of the three little war memorials-churches that were found in Thera and were dedicated to the worship of the dead who originated in the aristocracy. It is a second-century BC construction and on it the little Annunciation of the Virgin Mary church is erected.

Perissa is currently an important tourist resort of Santorini. On the tip of the beach rises the greyish figure of Mesa Vouno, the peak of which is accessible through a path. The little Katefiani church is perched in a concavity while on the strip which connects it with Prophet Elias the Ancient Thera cemeteries have been excavated. →

At the centre of the town the **Agora** is stretched which was divided into North and South sections. It was surrounded by private houses, public buildings and sanctuaries built in such a way so as to be prominent and at the same time not to obstruct the view across the sea.

The Royal Arcade, a big rectangular edifice with an interior colonnade, which constituted the centre of the town's public life and was built during the reign of Augustus (1st century BC), surrounds the Agora. Statues depicting members of the Cesar's family were placed on a specially arranged site on the northern section of the Arcade. On the northern segment of South Agora lies the little sanctuary of Dionysus, a construction of the Hellenistic Period (it consists of a vestibule and a cella while on its southeast, on a natural slope, stretch the ruins of the most important of the public buildings of Ancient Thera which was the **theatre** constructed under the Ptolemies (3rd century BC). Its orchestra was initially circular but certain works undertaken during the Roman Period (1st century AD) changed the stage's form which was expanded and occupied part of the orchestra. On a hewn rock there was a **Sanctuary** where the gods **Anoubis**, **Serapis** and **Isis**, Egyptian deities that came to Greece during the Hellenistic Period and the domination of the Ptolemies, were worshipped.

In the same area lay the **temple** of **Pythios Apollo**, important relics of which are preserved because on its site an early-Christian basilica was built. Another important temple in Ancient Thera was that of the **shrine** of **Artemidorus of Perge**, entirely hewn on a rock. It was founded in the end of the 4th or beginning of the 3rd century BC by Artemidorus himself, admiral of the Ptolemaic fleet, born in Perge of Asia Minor. On the

hewn façade of the rock there are the embossed symbols of the gods to whom the temple was dedicated. The eagle represents Zeus, the lion Apollo Stephaniforos (wreathed) and the dolphin Poseidon Pelagios (marine). Above the right-hand side of the Poseidon's dolphin lies the embossed wreathed head of Artemidorus. In this shrine the Cabiri, Dioscuri, Omonoia, Priapus and Hecate were also worshipped.

Finally, on the town's highest point, on the northwest of the Agora, lie the so-called Headquarters of the Ptolemaic guard. There is no difference between the building and any other private house but it was called Headquarters because of its strategic position. There is a gradient road leading to its courtyard. It consists of a series of rooms which border on three out of four sides of a square yard. Further on, there is another building, which consists of a big square yard with two closed spaces. Because of this arrangement it has been called the Gymnasium of the Guard. Most of the Ancient Thera houses were built along the eastern slope of the mountain. A lot of them had more than one floor. They were built with local lime and small irregular stones. The rooms were arranged around a closed courtyard and their interior was decorated with paintings. A necessary annex in every house was the cistern for the collection of rainwater. It was situated under the courtyard, the floor of which was the ceiling of the cistern.

Above: The houses and public buildings of the town were amphitheatrically built on the relatively level side of the mountain.

Left: On the hewn on a rock temple of Artemidorus Pergaeos there are the embossed symbols of the gods to whom it was dedicated. The eagle symbolizes Olympic Zeus and the lion Appolo Stefaniforos.

CASTLES AND
DEFENSIVE TOWERS

Above: The casteli of Akrotiri, the ruins of which lie almost in the centre of the homonymous village, was protected by a high wall which enclosed around twenty houses.

Below: The walls of the Niborio goulas, which is preserved in relatively good condition, remind us of the walls of the St. John monastery in Patmos.

antorini's beauty is not limited to the volcano and its antiquities. Castelia and goulades (castles and defensive towers), which stand semi-ruined on almost inaccessible locations, are attractions worth seeing. The Castelia are fortified villages where the houses were built on certain parts of their sides so as to create an unassailable exterior wall. When the guards gave the signal of danger, the inhabitants, including the serfs, found shelter here in order to escape from the incursions of the pirates who raided the Aegean. The history of Castelia is lost in the Middle Ages. In the 17th century, when we get for the first time a complete picture of the island, five castelia are mentioned. The most important one was **Skaros** of Castro (Greek for Castle). It was built under Imerovigli on the steep precipices of Theoskepasti. It took the invaders half an hour to reach its walls. A big bell situated on the top of the rock warned the inhabitants about the arrival of pirates. It was the capital of the island during the Frankish rule. It was the seat of the Catholics, the nobles of the island, the dignitaries as well as the seat of the Catholic bishop. In 1700, the population moved to Fira and its 200 houses, of which only ruins are currently preserved, were abandoned. The **Akrotiri** casteli, also called Pounda casteli (which means edge) lay almost at the centre of the homonymous village. It contained approximately 20 houses, of which we can only see ruins today. Above the main gate there is still the "hot", namely the hole wherefrom the inhabitants threw hot water in order to obstruct the entrance of pirates into the castle.

The **Emporeio** casteli dominated the region of the contemporary homonymous village. Emporeio (Emporium) or Niborio as its name

On the steep rock of Skaros was founded the castle that housed the medieval capital of the Venetians and the Latin population of Santorini. ←

indicates was Santorini's commercial centre. Within the casteli precincts there were about 80 houses that are now abandoned. The **Pyrgos** casteli, the so-called Kenourgioburgo, which means new castle, was a Byzantine construction and contained about 100 houses, two- and three-storeyed mansions, many of which were destroyed in the 1956 earthquake. It was the seat of the Ottoman Authorities' representative when he visited the island every two years to pass judgement on pending cases. Within the casteli there were four churches, St. James, St. John the Theologian, Holy Trinity and the well-known Theotokaki, a small domed square church decorated with hagiographies. It is said that it was built in the 10th century. Finally, there was the **Apanomeria** casteli, in comtemporary Oea, also called St. Nicholas castle. It is remarkable that outside the central gate of each casteli there was a church dedicated to St. Theodosia. Even in the Skaros casteli, the inhabitants of which were Catholics, the St. Theodosia church was present.

St. Theodosia who was seen as the patroness of the island's castelia must be St. Theodosia the iconolatric Saint who suffered martyrdom in 726 AD outside Chalki in Constantinople, during the years of iconoclast rule. Protection to the inhabitants was also offered by goulades, which were smaller isolated fortified constructions, defensive towers inside or outside the castelia. They were used by the castle owners and the serfs as dwelling and storage as well as refuges during the piratical assails.

Such goulades were situated: in **Fira**, built before the creation of the settlement, during the Ottoman rule by the Frankish family of Bozi in **Firostefani** (opposite the Skaros castle), the Delendas goulas in **Akrotiri** (in the middle of the casteli), the Dargenta family goulas in **Emporeio** (it was built in the periphery of the settlement and is preserved in rel-

The fortified casteli of Skaros hooked on the steep rocks of Theoskepaste were connected with the rest of the land through a bridge while the corner towers reinforced its strong walls

atively good condition until today) and in **Apono Meria**, in contemporary Oea near the casteli entrance –only its base is preserved. There were probably watch-towers as well on the island built in suitable elevations where the guards or sentries, who warned about the presence of pirates, lived. Perhaps, the name Imerovigli (Greek for day watch-tower) originates from this fact, as the Frank nobles who lived in Skaros had erected such an observation post on the Mesa Yialos side. Besides this watch-tower there must have been another one on the southern tip of the island, wherefrom the sentry could observe the south, across the Cretan Sea. The sentry was important. Therefore he was well rewarded. The money for his payment came from a special tax, the watch-tower tax (vigliatiko) that the inhabitants had to pay for the guard. The guard was a twenty-four hour duty. If the pirates approached the island during day-time, then the sentinels rang the watch-tower bell; if the attack took place during the night then they lit big fires. As soon as the alarm signal was given, the inhabitants began to hide in the castelia, goulades or any other natural improvised refuge. The latter served as refuges to the poor inhabitants who worked in the countryside, in the land of rich landowners.

As time passed and dangers from the sea ceased to exist, the Santorini inhabitants began to build outside the castelia and the newer settlements of the island were created which are distinguished for their simplicity, harmony and uniqueness.

The Niborio casteli was the centre of Santorini commercial life. The wall which protected it was formed by the outside walls of the last two-storeyed houses which left as an entrance to the interior three arched openings.

TRADITIONAL ARCHITECTURE:
SECULAR AND RELIGIOUS

The unique and unsurpassed in magnificence Santorini Landscape had a direct influence on the inhabitants' idiosyncrasy and subsequently to their architecture. Although the Santorini architecture belongs to the Aegean Sea architecture, nonetheless it presents peculiarities, which are due to the island's singular topographic and constructive conditions. The result was an architectural environment, the aesthetic values of which are very often praised.

The adaptation of the Santorini architecture to local construction materials is total. The black stone, red-, pumice stone and ash are the materials used for the construction of these shapes, which remind us of cubist creations and offer constantly new impressions to the visitor.

The roofs of the houses which are vaulted, either domical, barrel- or cross-vaulted, give to the Santorini architecture its particular character, the idiosyncratic technique and shapes which were incessantly evolving through the centuries. The application of vault-roofs was attributed to the effort of the locals to limit as much as possible the use of wood and used it only where it was absolutely necessary, for instance in doors, windows and their frames. Thus they spare construction timber which was practically non-existent on the island.

The houses in Oea, small all white, vaulted with openings on the side which faces the sea they are either hewn on the rock or built on it.

The idiosyncratic character of the Santorini architecture is completed with the hollowed-out houses dug in volcanic ash. This was an invention of the lower classes in order to ensure easy and chiefly cheap shelter.

In their current form, the island's settlements are situated either on the edge of the precipice towards the caldera (Fira, Oea, Therasia), or orig-

inate in the development of the castelia settlements outside the walls (Pyrgos, Niborio, Akrotiri) or they are hollowed-out and follow the beds of a torrent stretching on the major area (Vothonas, Finikia, Karterados).

As for their construction, the Santorini houses are divided into three types. These are: hollowed-out or dug (being hewn on the vertical front of the ash layer), semi-built (with a part of their construction built usually on the access side and the rest being hollowed-out) and in built ones which are normally built on the ground.

THE HOLLOWED-OUT HOUSES

The hollowed-out houses are the simplest forms of house construction on the island. They were usually home to very poor people as their construction was in fact inexpensive. They are long and the narrow façade is the only visible side of the hollowed-out construction. This oblong construction has a cylindrical roof made of the hewing of some volcanic material. Sometimes the house consists of a single room (single-roomed). But usually a built wall separates it in two smaller rooms (two-roomed). The front room (which was called salon) was used as a living room and the rear one as a bedroom. On the built side, besides the door which lies in the middle, there are three more openings (two windows on the right- and left-hand sides, respectively, and a big rectangular fanlight) which were normally repeated on the interior separating wall, ensuring thus light and air to the rear room. The kitchen and the fireplace, a built vault niche, communicate with the living room while the water-closet lies in a small yard where also the cistern lies, a necessary annex to every house for the collection of the rain-water, given that Santorini as the rest of the Cyclades islands is arid.

When the family needs require it, the two-roomed hollowed-out house can have a twin one, namely exactly beside it they construct a copy of their house which is used either as a secondary or as a main house. In this case access to the house interior is effected through the small front yard. Sometimes the singularity of the soil permits the farming of land above the hollowed-out houses.

On the **semi-built** houses, the sheltering of the built sections was vault of cross-vault-made of a molten casting mixture of stones and ash.

Finally, the **built** houses are either single- (mainly those outside the villages) or two-roomed. The two-roomed ones are often twins and sometimes, if the owners are rich or intend to give the upper floor as a dowry, two-storeyed. They have a little yard to which they give both the main and the auxiliary rooms such as the kitchen, the oven, the water-closet and the stable. Their walls are built with local stones and plastered while the sheltering is done through cylindrical or domical vaults.

The Santorini houses are divided into three groups as per their type: rural, popular-urban and mansions.

The **rural** house is usually situated on the outskirts of a settlement where there is enough space or in the fields. Depending on its position it might be hollowed-out or built. It has necessarily a spacious yard and a series of auxiliary annexes around the main house. It also has a subterranean cistern for the collection of rainwater, which consists of the tank and the "koundouta", the pipes that bring the rainwater into the cistern.

Due to the long tradition of Santorini in wine production, there are areas where almost every rural house has a kanava, wine producing and storing facilities. The kanava with the typical arched door contains two wine-presses, a cistern as well as the casks which are filled with sweet local wine. Usually the kanava is hollowed-out but it has an opening, called anemoloos, as ventilation for the vapours when the must begins to ferment.

The **urban – popular** house is situated at the centre of the densely inhabited Santorini settlements. Usually it has a limited free space, irregular form because of the adjoining properties and less space for domestic animals than the rural houses. It is normally multi-storeyed with the auxiliary rooms lying in different levels compared to the main house. The furniture is limited to the absolutely necessary pieces, namely chests for the storing of cloths and food and those pieces that were widely used in the Aegean with the development of shipping, namely tables, sofas and buffets which were initially used only by the upper class.

The mansions as well as the popular – urban houses are also situated at the central areas of the settlements. Perhaps, the mansions initially resembled the contemporary urban – popular houses because both of them were evolved from the castelia houses. Their main charac-

Images such as this of the coloured yard door which is framed by an all white wall are frequent in the alleys of Santorini settlements. The wall looks even whiter under the brightness of the Aegean light.

teristics, through which are known to us today, namely the imposing monolithic shape and their symmetric monumental façades, must have been acquired in later periods. The monumental mansion appeared in Santorini in the mid-nineteen century as a result of the appearance of a thriving shipowning commercial class. In Oea, there is a special quarter containing exclusively the ship-owners' mansions, called Sideras built in the end of the 19th and beginning of the 20th centuries. The mansions are situated on the level side of the precipice where construction is sparse while on the densely constructed side of the precipice lie the hollowed-out houses of the ship-crews.

Also in Messaria the central part is occupied by large estates that belonged to local wealthy families.

THE CHURCHES OF SANTORINI

The churches of Santorini, like its houses, form a cubist architectural complex. The sites chosen for churches are most of the times adequate as for their orientation space economy and firm foundations but they are not chosen to highlight the architectural designs. The artisans tried to highlight them either with a yard, a road extension or by making a nice bell-tower. Until the 1956 earthquakes Santorini had 260 churches. This great number is due to the intense religious feeling of the islanders during the years of the Frankish rule, which was developed as a reaction to Catholicism.

The island's churches are divided into hollowed-out and built. The hollowed-out ones (which are 1/5 of the total) are small in size and sim-

The blue elegant dome and the slender bell tower decorate uniquely the built churches of Santorini.

ple while the sanctuary is not very well oriented. They belong to the architectural type of the single-aisled basilica with a hewn on the rock cylindrical dome. Hollowed-out churches are the Virgin Mary Sergena in Vothonas, St. Anthony in Imerovigli, St. John in Mylonades etc. But most of the island's churches are built. In these churches the local artisans managed to keep alive the traditions against the Roman-catholic rule. Therefore even the elements borrowed by Occidental art were assimilated in a creative and free manner. The built churches usually belong to the single-aisled basilica type with a marble roof or dome and often with the annex of a chapel. The two-aisled basilicas are considerably less (five in total), the older one of which is St. Irini in Perissa, most likely built in the 12th century. Some others are of the cross-inscribed type with a dome, only three are square with a dome (the most typical is Theotokaki in Pyrgos), while a great number belongs to the cross-vault type. The dome is either white as the entire church is, or azure. Often it is pleated. Many times a purely Renaissance element is added: the dome is completed by a prominence like a second dome on which the cross is standing. The façade of some churches is dominated by two bell-towers, as it is common in cathedrals.

Beside the church, even if it is a hollowed-out one, there is often a large room called "festival room". In there the food is prepared, which is destined for the believers after the mass during the Saint's festival.

There are currently about 350 churches in Santorini, big and small, chapels and country-churches. This fact which is reinforced by the presence of many private churches indicates the great piety of the islanders.

The biggest private churches are these of St. Artemios, which belongs to the Belonias family, past Imerovigli as we head towards Oea, St. Epiphanios of the Alifrangis family on the central square of Akrotiri and Sts. Anargyroi of the Syrigos family in Megalochori. A remarkable little church is St. Barbara of the M. Danezis family in Mesaria, which lay in the courtyard of the "St. Barbara Eye-clinic" that functioned from 1929 until 1954 on the island.

Many temples built in Santorini after the fall of Constantinople to the Turks in 1453 constitute art monuments made by local artisans. Among these monuments are included the two hollowed-out churches of St. Anthony and St. George in Imerovigli, and St. John Theologian in Kato Fira (1539-1650), the Virgin Mary Gardiotissa and the Transfiguration (built in the end of the 16th century) in Exo Gonia, the Archangels (1653) in Mesa Gonia and the Presentation of the Virgin Mary in the Temple (1660-1661) in Pyrgos. These churches are decorated with portable icons painted by Cretan as well as by local hagiographers who followed the Cretan-Venetian School.

MILLS AND BAKERIES

The picture of the mill standing against the wind is a familiar one in Cyclades. It is also present in Santorini.

We rarely meet a house-mill namely a mill and a bakery at the same time where bread and flour are supplied to the neighbouring settlement. In such a case the bakery which was a continuation of the baker's house was subterranean so as not to obstruct the mill's function.

Usually the mills were isolated constructions built outside the inhabited areas, in windward sites. In Megalochori, Niborio and Akrotiri lie most of the Santorini mills which are round with an articulated straw-made roof. The mill wheel with the sails turned with every wind and moved the upper mill-stone. Barley and the rest of cereals were ground through the friction of the upper mill-stone to the low one.

TOURING AROUND
THE ISLAND

Our acquaintance with contemporary Santorini will start from its capital, **Fira**, which is one of the most crowded tourist settlements.

Fira will be our starting point for our excursions to the most important regions of the island.

The history of the town begins after 1700. It was around this date that the piratical incursions were reduced and the inhabitants of Skaros decided to abandon the strong castle and settle lower, on a site with access to the sea. Thus, they chose this site, high on the middle of the island's western coast. Here, along the caldera edge unfold the picturesque quarters of the small town. The landscape seen from here is unique: opposite stands the volcano, in the background looms Therasia, further right Oea and further on the left-hand side the southern edge of Santorini. This fascinating view in combination with the architectural style of the settlement (in spite of the alterations suffered during the last years by newer constructions) make Fira one of the most breathtaking sites in Greece.

← *As night falls Fira is covered by the dim colours of dusk.*

Many of the old hollowed-out houses, dug inside the soft rock and hooked on the edge of the cliff are currently renovated. Some of them function as restaurants, cafeterias, bar and discos.

The blue domes of the churches in Fira have as a background the dark blue waters of the caldera which is stretched in front of them.

Nowadays, Fira is evolved into a crowded tourist resort with many hotels and rooms to let, dozens of tavernas, bars, cafeterias or discos as well as with shops selling popular art items (ceramics, hand-woven textiles) souvenirs and expensive jewelry. The little town, which lies 260 meters above sea level, is crossed by four central, almost parallel to each other streets, intersected by vertical parallel alleys. Cars are prohibited

in these streets with the exception of 25th March Street. At about the centre of the 25th March the street widens and a small rectangular square is formed, the Thetokopoulos square. From this point the Danezis street starts which will lead us to the pebble-paved Marinatos street. Descending the wide stairs we meet a sinuous cobbled-road which leads to the coast in Mesa Yalos or Fira bay. Here lay in the past the harbour of Santorini before it was moved to Athinios. Currently only cruise-ships moor here. But they anchor off the mole and moor on the buoys which are scattered within the caldera since its depth does not allow any kind of ship to drop anchor. From Yalos, donkeys go uphill and transport locals and tourists alike to Fira, unless the latter prefer to take the funicular or walk. We are again in Fira. We head towards the southern part of the town through one of the central roads, the Ipapandi Street. We leave the crowded stores with the colourful stock behind and reach the Orthodox cathedral of the island, the Presentation or Virgin Mary of Belonias with the imposing bell-tower and the long arcade. The view from this point is fascinating. We stare at the deep blue waters of the caldera, while further downhill, the lines of white houses go downward following the declivity of the cliff. We can discern the narrow cobbled roads as

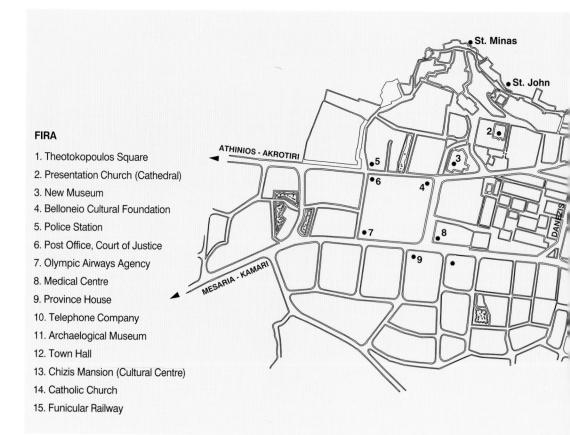

FIRA

1. Theotokopoulos Square
2. Presentation Church (Cathedral)
3. New Museum
4. Belloneio Cultural Foundation
5. Police Station
6. Post Office, Court of Justice
7. Olympic Airways Agency
8. Medical Centre
9. Province House
10. Telephone Company
11. Archaelogical Museum
12. Town Hall
13. Chizis Mansion (Cultural Centre)
14. Catholic Church
15. Funicular Railway

they twist and mix with the small yards. The buildings look as if they are leaning towards each other in a desperate effort to find some free space. What is a house's yard is at the same time another's terrace. We see the level surfaces mingling with the curves of domes and vaults, the 'infinite' white 'interrupted' here and there by the azure of a church or the ochre of a house.

Heading downhill to Fira, to the southerly quarter of the town and lower on the cliff, we meet the St. George church and further on the picturesque all-white St. Menas church with the typical Santorini double dome. In Kato Fira we will see one more church, the church of Christ with a chiselled iconostasis and an Episcopal throne.

We leave Kato Fira and the southern part of the little town. We head towards its northern edge –which currently almost joins the next settlement, Firostefani- going uphill through the Ipapandi Street where dozens of stores are situated. We enter the alleys, which are here and there covered by arches and cross-vaults. Shops border on cafés, bars and restaurants. Where Ypapandis Street ends lies the Archaeological Museum with the great palm-tree decorating its garden and further north on the corner of Ayiou Ioannou Street (the central road of the Catholic

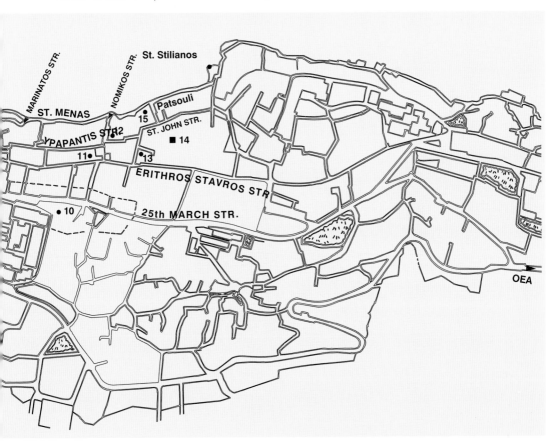

BUOYS

Cruise-ships reaching the island moor in Fira bay. But they anchor off the mole and moor on the buoys which

are scattered within the caldera since its depth does not allow any kind of ship to drop anchor.

← **Ypapandi or Panayia of Belonias with the magnificent dome and the high bell tower is the orthodox cathedral of Santorini.**

Below:
A big earthenware jar of the Archaic Era with an embossed decoration of a swan on the neck and chariots drawn by flying horses lower.

Right:
Statuette of Aphrodite who ties her sandal.

Fira, Archaeological Museum.

quarter) and Erythrou Stavrou Street lies the Ghizis mansion. In the Catholic quarter we will see the monastery of the Sisters of Mercy who came to Thera in 1841. We will also see the convent of the Dominican nuns and beside it its church, Rodario, a construction which represents the influence of baroque on local architecture as well as the Catholic cathedral called Dome with its high bell-tower and finally, the Lazaristes monastery and its church. In the Dominican Sisters convent, there is a school of carpet-making of the Greek Organization of Arts and Crafts where hand-woven carpets are manufactured. As we stare at the sea, we will discern, hooked on the edge of the cliff the little St. Stylianos church and further left we will find ourselves in Patsouli, the most prominent point of Fira with the breathtaking views across the caldera, the little Mesa Yalos harbour and the road heading uphill to reach the capital of the island.

While we are in Fira, a visit to the **Archaeological Museum** is worth taking, which houses the finds from the Akrotiri and Mesa Vouno excavations.

In its halls we will see:
-Pots and statuettes of the Early Cycladic period (2500-2000 BC)
-Pots from Akrotiri
-Geometrical and Attic pots and statuettes of the 8th and 7th centuries BC
-Sculptures of the Archaic, Hellenistic and Roman periods

In the **Ghizis** mansion, where the Thera Cultural Centre is housed, there is an exhibition of icons, documents, maps, paintings and other relics relative to Santorini while during the summer the mansion accommodates various cultural events.

More exhibitions, congresses, concerts, conferences and other events are housed in the **Petros Nomikos** Congress Centre.

KOLUMBO

OEA

IMEROVIGLI

VOURVOULOS

FIROSTEFANI

KONDOCHORI

FIRA

1ST ITINERARY:

FIROSTEFANI, IMEROVIGLI,

OEA, VOURVOULOS, KONDOCHORI

We have left Fira behind. About 800 hundred meters further, we meet **Firostefani**. It is built on the caldera precipices and offers to those who visit it excellent views across the sea and Kamenes.

We meet again the same scenery: White houses struggling to hang on to almost vertical caldera inner sides which immerse in the deep blue waters. Cobbled roads, restaurants, cafés, bars, pubs, hotels, a picturesque square and the St. Gerasimos church, the only one with cypresses on the island. Further on, on our right-hand side facing the sea, rises the steep dark rock of Skaros, while a little bit further we can barely see the white figure of the Theoskepasti little church resting on the brownish stones.

En route from Firostefani to Imerovigli, we will meet the old Orthodox convent of **St. Nicholas**, founded in 1651 by the Chizi family. It was removed from its original site in Skaros between 1819 and 1821. The katholikon (main church) of the monastery is triune, namely each of the three chapels is dedicated to a different saint: St. Panteleimonas, Zoodochos Pighi and St. Nicholas. It contains a valuable chiselled iconostasis in the katholikon and a Byzantine icon of St. Nicholas.

Our next stop is **Imerovigli**. Its name dates obviously from the years of pirates and must mean day observation post. Indeed, from this point, which is the highest point of the caldera, the view is fascinating. The bare red and black earth meets the deep blue seawaters. The wild natural beauty is perfectly balanced by the grace and serenity bestowed upon local architecture by the use of curves. We can find hotels, restaurants and nightclubs as well as the Virgin Mary of Malta church,

which was rebuilt after the 1956 earthquakes. From the old temple on-ly the fine chiselled icon-screen is preserved which depicts scenes from the Old Testament.

A narrow track starts from Imerovigli and leads through uphill and downhill turns to Skaros, the most important castle of Santorini during the Frankish rule built by Marco Sanudo in 1207 (See p. 30).

Leaving Imerovigli, we head towards the northern tip of the island, which gradually lowers until it reaches the open sea. The greenish or yellowish land-plots look like parallelogram strips interrupted here and there by rows of little white houses.

On a certain spot of our itinerary we have the feeling that we domi-nate this particularly strange landscape. The views to our right- and left-hand sides reach the land-plots and further on touch the open sea and the caldera respectively.

Some 11 kilometers from Fira lies **Oea**, perhaps the most picturesque settlement of Santorini, which was the island's commercial centre un-til the Second World War.

It stares at the Therasia islet exactly opposite. It is also called Ano Meria and consists of six quarters: Oea proper, the rural **Perivolas**, almost adjoining Oea, the traditional **Finikia** with many churches, farm-hous-es and the cave of Our Lady Chochlideri on the left-hand side of the

The green terraced plots of land in the plain which are stretching to the northeast of Oea, follow the shape of the soil which gradually descends and reaches the open sea.

road that joins the church to Oea, **Tholos** and finally, on the base of the caldera the harbours **Ammoudi** and **Armeni**. There is mention of Oea long before 1650. During the Frankish rule it was the capital of one of the five administrative districts to which Santorini was divided. Oea thrived in the end of the 19th and the beginning of the 20th centuries. Its prosperity was based on the fleet created by its inhabitants for the transportation of goods in East Mediterranean and mainly between Alexandria and Russia. In 1890, it had around 2,500 inhabitants and 130 ships while a small shipyard was established in Armeni. It had 13 parishes, a bank, customs and artisan workshops. Equally thriving was the local agriculture.

The imposing mansions of the inhabitants, some of which are preserved and constitute real jewels for the village, offer additional evidence for the richness accumulated in the area. Nowadays Oea is the second-biggest settlement of the island. It is like Fira lineally developed on the edge of the cliff, along the axis of a central marble-paved road. Its quarters are divided into: the shipmasters' quarter which contains mansions of the end of the 19th and beginning of 20th centuries, in a Renaissance style with neoclassical influences as well as with local elements; the crews' quarter, on the caldera precipice with chiefly hollowed-out houses densely built; the Perivolas rural quarter and finally the post-earthquake quarter which contains houses built after the 1956 earthquake to shelter the homeless.

A number of Oea old buildings (about 60) are remarkably restored and

Ammoudi is one of Oea's harbours. Its buildings were used by the inhabitants of Apanomeria for the storing of the merchandise from their boats.

A terraced paved road leads to the second harbour, Armeni, after 286 stairs which wind on the caldera steep sides.

transformed into inns by G.N.T.O. As we wander through the cobbled roads of the little town, we see old houses of a unique plasticity, domes of churches, the white, blue and ochre composing a picture of impressive beauty.

Doors and yards adorned with flowers, staircases, and terraces appear unexpectedly projected on the deep blue of the sea and create a harmonious picture drenched in the dazzling sunshine of the Aegean. We walk through narrow alleys and when we have the impression that we are reaching a dead-end they turn abruptly and lead us to a traditional house, a terrace-passage or to the edge of the cliff. The sunset from this relatively quiet village offers a unique feeling as the sun fades away inside the dark seawaters.

Although Oea is built, like the three previously mentioned settlements, along the caldera precipices it lies near the sea because the cliffs are lower in this point. Two sinuous cobbled roads, with 286 and 214 stairs lead to Armeni and Ammoudi, respectively. There is also an asphalt road leading to Ammoudi.

The small settlements we are about to meet here constitute, like all the other Santorini settlements, spectacular architectural complexes char-

Above, left: From the Oea goulas which was rising past the entrance of the St. Nicholas casteli only the base is preserved. From this point the sunset is unique.

acterized by the variety of shapes, the plasticity of buildings and their harmonious composition. In the olden days, the inhabitants used the Ammoudi buildings as storing facilities for goods due to be loaded on or unloaded from ships.

On the small 'arm' that separates the two little bays, on a rocky islet, is perched as if it were hewn on the rock, the little white church of St. Nicholas, patron saint of the seamen.

Armeni and Ammoudi are ideal for swimming while beside Armeni lies Armenaki and further north from Ammoudi, lies the Katharos beach with the black stones and the corroded rocks which give the impression of a moonscape.

Oea, although it lacks the noisy character of Fira, nonetheless has hotels, stores, restaurants, bars, discos, tavernas and cafeterias.

Below, left: Water colour depicting a sailing boat from Oea Nautical Museum.

Among the numerous churches of Oea, we will see the restored tiny church of Zoodochos Peghe in the Goulas area and at the entrance of the Perivolas neighbourhood the also restored mill of Panais with a straw-roof and sails.

Before leaving the settlement, we must visit the **Nautical Museum**, which is housed in a restored two-storeyed neoclassical mansion on the village's central road. Its halls contain figure-heads, nautical chests, navigation instruments, models of ships, water-colours etc. Moreover, on the same road beside the G.N.T.O. reception office lies the weaving-mill. It is used for the production of textiles as well as for training.

We leave Oea and return to Fira through a different route. The road heads in the beginning northwards then eastwards and finally takes a turn southwards and runs along the eastern coastline of the island.

Past Oea, in a 3-kilometer distance we will meet the **Baxedes** site and the wide homonymous beach, further east the **Kolumbo** cape and its blackish sandy beach – there, off shore and inside the sea, lies the homonymous crater which erupted in 1650 BC - and further south **Pori** and its little harbour with the fishing-boats.

Next we meet the settlement of **Vourvoulos**, with a traditional local colour and views across the open sea. It is situated only 5 kilometers outside Fira while the left-hand side turn of the crossroad we meet before entering the village leads to the Vourvoulos beach.

Past Vourvoulos we meet **Kondochori**. Here there is a folk art museum, which includes among its exhibits workshops of old professions, a hollowed-out house, a distillery etc. When the main road forks, a fork leads to a beach, called Apoxo Yalos or Pegadia, which is stretched 1,5 kilometer to the east of the main road. Kondochori is situated in a one-kilometer distance from Fira, where our first Santorini itinerary ends.

Below:
On the edge of the cliff the white houses of Oea have been developed. Down to the coast, as small white nests, we can distinguish Ammoudi and Armeni, while on the islet which lies between them the St. Nicholas country church is situated.

FIRA

KARTERADOS

MONOLITHOS

MESARIA

VOTHONAS

MESA GONIA

KAMARI

MESA VOUNO

2ND ITINERARY:

KARTERADOS, MONOLITHOS, MESARIA,
VOTHONAS, PANAGIA PISKOPI GONIAS,
KAMARI, MESA VOUNO (ANCIENT THERA)

Our second itinerary aims at getting acquainted with the part of the island, which lies on the south and southeast of Fira. We will visit Karterados, Monolithos, Kamari and arrive at Mesa Vouno where the Ancient Thera ruins are situated.

A little out of town (about 1,5 kilometer) we meet the crossroads which will lead us to **Karterados**, a traditional village built on the slopes of a gully so as to give the impression of being half-buried in the ground. It contains three important churches: the Ascension which has two bell-towers that dominate its entrance and is painted, in contrast to the other two, ochre while the St. Nicholas church with the slender palm-trees and the Presentation of the Virgin Mary are all white.

From Karterados the road heads to Exo Yalos of Karterados, a picturesque beach with black pebbles and sand.

Returning from Exos Yalos of Karterados, we take the road leading to **Monolithos**. The rock, which rises beside the asphalt and shelters at its foot the white church of St. John, is like Profitis Ilias and Mesa Vouno a relic of Aegeida.

While we are in Monolithos, we can swim in the beach with the fine sand which is called Limani, while further north another beach awaits us, the Yalos Vardou. It is easy to go to Kamari from Monolithos if we follow the asphalt road, which after bypassing the little St. John church runs parallel to the airport.

Returning to the main road, we will make a small detour and pause shortly in **Messaria** (4 km southeast of Fira) which is built in an area with vines. Here, a great part of local wine is produced. We will meet

houses hollowed-out on the rock and imposing mansions. We will also see the lily-white St. Spyridon church, a single-aisled domed basilica with a smaller dome on top of the first one, and the St. Demetrios church with a white dome and a façade which resembles a mosaic because it is made of small coloured stones. In Mesaria we will find hotels, bars, restaurants, cafeterias, and tavernas. Near Mesaria, 2 km to the south, lies **Vothonas** which almost joins it, half-hidden on the torrent sides with the beautiful houses and hollowed-out, hewn on caves churches such as the Virgin Mary of Sergina and the Virgin Mary of Trypa.

Past Mesaria and Vothonas, our next stop in this itinerary is the picturesque **Mesa Gonia** or **Episkopi Gonias**, the main animal-rearing village of Santorini. Near Mesa Gonia but further north lies **Exo Gonia**, another small settlement with the St. Charalambous church dominating the elevation. Mesa and Exo Gonia are typical farming villages where almost every house is equipped with facilities for the production and storing of wine. About 700 meters outside the Mesa Gonia village, on a Profitis Ilias slope, the **Virgin Mary Piskopi Gonias** is built which is the most important Byzantine monument on the island. Its festival is on the 15th August. The Byzantine temple was erected on the site of one of the three basilicas of the island. It was a three-aisled, domed, with five columns in each colonnade basilica arguably built in the end of the 6th or the beginning of the 7th century BC. The temple we see today

Mesaria, one of the picturesque settlements of Santorini.

must have been founded on the basilica ruins between 1081 and 1118 by emperor Alexios I Comnenos, according to an inscription which was located in the past above the southern door of the nave: "Alexios Comnenos, loyal king, by Christ emperor of Romans". This Byzantine temple, which belongs to the cross-inscribed domed type and is called Piskopi (Greek for diocese) of Santorini, or Our Lady of Piskopi or Virgin Mary of Gonia, was originally the katholikon of a monastery as well as the bishopric seat of Santorini. When in 1207 the Franks arrived at the island, it was granted to the Catholics. During the Ottoman rule it was used by both dogmas (Orthodox and Catholic) a fact that resulted in disputes for the exclusive use of the church. This situation ended in 1768 when it was granted to the Orthodox community. The orig-

inal building has undergone various alterations and a number of annexes such as the outside staircase and the bell-tower. It contains a valuable marble iconostasis while the murals date from about 1100. After our visit to Piskopi Gonias, we take the road to **Kamari**, the modern tourist resort with the vast beach. Here we will find one of the most popular beaches of Santorini with black pebbles and sand, with deep crystal clear waters. It lies about 10 km from Fira.

Kamari, which functioned in the Historic Period as the harbour of Ancient Thera and was called Oea, is a modern settlement developed during the last decades along with the tourist development of the entire island. It has many hotels, restaurants, pubs, cafeterias, bars, discotheques and tavernas. In Kamari operates the winepress of the Volcan Company founded in 1880. In its premises it houses a museum where machinery, implements and utensils relative to the wine production are exhibited. From Kamari a sinuous road surrounded by shadowy pine-trees brings us after 3km to Mesa Vouno where the ruins of Ancient Thera are situated. The view from the entrance of the archaeological site is panoramic and fascinating. Staring at the four points of the compass we can discern low to the north Kamari and the narrow stone-built road that brought us here winding on the mountain's steep slopes, on the south Perisa and the track heading downhill to the beach while on the west we see another track unfolding and leading to Profitis Ilias. Our itinerary ends in Ancient Thera (see p. 55), the most important town of Santorini in the Historic Years.

Near Mesaria lies Vothonas with its typical hollowed out houses.

Kamari with the endless beach is a modern tourist resort which during the summer swarms with bathers who enjoy the bright sun and the clean sea. →

FIRA

PYRGOS

PROFITIS ILIAS

3RD ITINERARY:

PYRGOS, PROPHET ELIAS MONASTERY

In our third excursion in Santorini we will visit **Pyrgos** the large inland village which is stretched to the southeast of Fira in a 7,5-kilometer distance. It is a model of fortified settlement and is unique in Santorini for its medieval characteristics. Its houses are amphitheatrically built and embrace the slope of the low elevation from where we can have excellent views across the entire island. On the top of the hill and around it the medieval castle was built which was one of Thera's five castles during the Frankish rule. The exterior walls of private houses formed part of the settlement's fortification. Between the houses we can distinguish the domes and bell-

Built on an elevation, Pyrgos which is known for its numerous churches owes its name to the medieval castle that dominated the hill's peak.

towers of the village's numerous churches. One of them is the Dormition of the Virgin Mary church known as Theotokaki, a small square domed church, one of the oldest of Santorini. It was probably built in the 10th or 11th century. Its interior decoration dates from the 14th century and contains a chiselled iconostasis and precious icons. There is also a museum in the Pyrgos castle where icons from local churches are exhibited. Before leaving Pyrgos, we can visit the wine-press of the Santo Company, which houses an exhibition with local products. Outside the village (4km) on the top of **Profitis Ilias** (Prophet Elias), 565 meters above sea level, we will see the homonymous male monastery. Its compact figure resembles a fort. Its entrance is dominated by the white silhouette of the tiny St. Nektarios church. The monastery was founded in 1711 and its erection was completed in two stages. The first one started in March 1711 and lasted until May 1724 and the second one comprised the period from November 1852 to March 1857. It contains a valuable richly decorated chiselled iconostasis inside the katholikon made in 1836. In the past, the Profitis Ilias monastery was very prosperous. It possessed a mercantile ship that traded to the monastery's profit. At the same time, it was a centre of spiritual and national activities. From 1806 until 1845 there functioned a school for the education of Greek children. It is also worth visiting the monastery's museum, which houses its relics. The museum has a folkloric collection that consists of traditional pieces of furniture, implements, hand-woven textiles, pieces of embroidery and porcelains.

The Prophet Elias monastery, the compact figure of which reminds us of a castle, founded in 1711.

The contemporary settlement of Pyrgos preserves many medieval elements. Between the white houses the blue domes and the white bell towers of its churches are distinguished. In the background we can discern Skaros, Fira and the dark waters of caldera. →

4TH ITINERARY:

ATHINIOS, MEGALOCHORI,
NIBORIO, PERISSA, AKROTIRI

I n the fourth itinerary in Santorini we will get to know the rest of its southern part. We will visit Niborio and Perissa and finally, Akrotiri.

Following the main road with the shadowy slender eucalyptuses on both sides, which crosses the island from north to south, about 7,5 km from Fira we will meet a crossroad. From there a sinuous road leads after 3,5 km to **Athinios** the harbour of Santorini where ferry-boats moor. The settlement consists of a few houses and restaurants while on the right-hand side of the mole we can see a small pebbly beach.

Athinios, which lies almost in the middle of the caldera coast, is the harbour of Santorini where boats that arrive in the island berth.

We leave Athinios and head uphill towards the main road. We soon reach **Megalochori**. It is an inland village and one of the few traditional villages of Santorini that did not undergo substantial changes. In its narrow alleys and cobbled streets hollowed-out houses coexist harmoniously with mansions and lily-white churches, which bear the mark of the Aegean art. Here we will see the Presentation of the Virgin Mary church, which contains a chiselled iconostasis, and an ornate calendarium. There is also the wine-press of Boutaris Company where beside the various programmes of wine-testing and the presentations of the island's history, you can taste the wines produced by the company. Past Megalochori we meet **Emborio** or **Niborio**, a southern large village with narrow alleys and picturesque houses. Built in the middle of a fertile plain, it was one of the five castles of the island during the Frankish rule as well as the centre of commercial activity (see p. 76). A relic of that period is the goulas, which is preserved in relatively good condition. On the mountain opposite the village, we can discern the lonely shapes of the windmills, which in the past swarmed with life. Its harbour is Perissa which lies in a two-kilometer distance from the village and the inhabitants of Niborio were the only islanders who were mainly employed in fishing. Outside Niborio one of the war-memorials of Ancient Thera, which was dedicated to the worship of dead of aristocratic origin. The building formed part of the ancient sanctuary of the goddess Basileia and was constructed in the 3rd century BC. On top of it the little St. Nicholas Marmaritis (made of marble) church is built which took its name from the grey hewn marble that was used to construct the ancient sanctuary. To the east of Niborio (3km) lie **Perissa** and its extensive beach which together with Kamari are the most popular destinations of Santorini. As soon as we arrive here

Emporio is built in the middle of a fertile plain. Near it we can discern Perissa with the beautiful beach.

we have a strong desire to swim in the clear waters and rest on the beautiful sandy beach with the fine black sand. Its northern tip is protected by the steep and grey southern slopes of Mesa Vouno, on a side of which the little country-church of Virgin Mary Katefiani (or Katefchiani) stands staring at the Perissa coast. From Perissa a narrow track heads upwards to the rocky elevation and reaches Mesa Vouno. The coastal settlement of Perissa, with the hotels, restaurants and all kinds of clubs, competes with Kamari. Among the white buildings of the settlement, the white figure of the Holy Cross church is distinguished on the seaside. On the site that the contemporary imposing temple, the biggest on the island, rises, there was a five-domed octagonal church built between 1835-1840 which was destroyed by the 1956 earthquakes. The older temple was erected in 1835 on the site where a bronze cross and a Virgin icon were found inside a vaulted-tomb on the suggestion of a peasant from Episkopi Gonias. Beside Perissa, ideal for swimming are the Perivolos and Ai-Giorgis Thalassinos beaches as well as the Exomytis beach with the shallow waters. If you want to go there, take the coastal road which starts from Perissa and reaches Vlychada where there is a beach with various coloured volcanic rocks. We leave Perissa, bypass Niborio and return to the main road that heads to the most southerly part of Santorini, following the caldera coasts. The next and last stop of this itinerary is

Near Akrotiri lies the special beach of Kokkini Ammos or Kokkini Paralia. The peculiar red and black rocks 'descend' almost vertically to the dark-coloured beach.

Akrotiri, a picturesque village with narrow streets, white houses and a deserted goulas, which lies in a seven- and fifteen-kilometer distance from Athinio and Fira, respectively. Here there was situated another of the castelia during the Frankish rule, which repelled the Turkish raids courageously until 1617 (see p. 76). Akrotiri is built on a hillside. Some 1,000 meters outside the village lies the important archaeological site with the finds from the prehistoric town (see p. 33). A little out of the archaeological site the beach of the village is stretched while if we continue for some 700 m to the west, we will meet the Mavro Rachidi site. Here, on the red and black rocks of lava hurled out of the volcano we will see the little white church of St. Nicholas. Tradition has it that a shipmaster set forth a journey with his ship. At a certain moment his ship was immobilized. Then the captain thought that someboidy of his crew had committed a sin. Indeed, one of his sailors had stolen an icon of St. Nicholas. The captain fearing the

anger of the Saint, took the icon broke it into two pieces and threw them in the sea. Then the boat started to move again. Soon the icon was found in front of the St. Nicholas country-church. This story is related to many old legends that people tell with slight variations. During the Classical years boats were immobilized by a wonder-making fish while during the Middle Ages by a Gorgon. After a ten-minute eastward walk from the St. Nicholas country-church we reach the beautiful beach Kokkini Ammos (Red Sand) or Kokkini Paralia (Red Beach) with the characteristic red and black rocks which descend vertically upon a wonderful beach. Further west from Kokkini Ammos another beach is stretched, the Lefki Paralia (White Beach). We will reach this point by caiques from Akrotiri. From Akrotiri the road continues westwards and after 5 kilometers reaches the outermost point of Santorini, the Akrotiri cape. As we go further, the caldera lies on our right-hand side while traffic signs indicate the points wherefrom the bypassing secondary roads start which lead to the Kambia and Mesa Pigadia beaches. At the end of the itinerary we see **Faros** (Lighthouse) which rises majestically on the edge of the precipitous rocks while the azure Aegean embraces it.

The all white church of the patron saint of the seamen, St. Nicholas harmonically matches the red and black rocks.

The Perissa beach with the fine black sand and crystal clean waters constitutes one of the most popular and crowded beaches of Santorini.

→

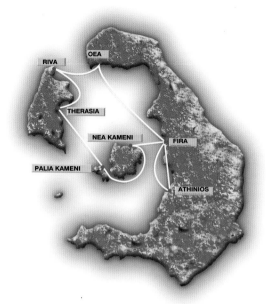

5TH ITINERARY:

NEA KAMENI (VOLCANO),
PALEA KAMENI, THERASIA

With this itinerary we will conclude our acquaintance with the island of Santorini. In this excursion we will not use a car, instead we will descend from Fira to Mesa Yalos and take a small boat which will carry us to Nea and Palia Kameni and finally to Therasia. The small ferry-boat from Athinios follows the same itinerary, from Athinios, to Mesa Yalos, from there to Nea and Palia Kameni, Therasia, Oea and back to Athinios. Nea Kameni is a mass of dark-coloured material, which is nothing but petrified lava hurled out of the bowels of the earth in a viscous form. On its top lies the crater of the currently active volcano while some other smaller concavities appear in various points of its surface.

The dominant grey-black colour, the lack of any form of vegetation, the rugged terrain made of black lava rocks, the gaping "openings" here and there bring to mind moonscape pictures and lead us to retrace the conditions under which this idiosyncratic island was formed.

The boats leave us in the small bay of Peroulio. The dark grey and black stones we are stepping on are made of the lava, which created Mikri Kameni. Before we set for the volcano peak, we can stare at Santorini. The rock of Skaros and the caldera inner sides with the white houses of Fira, Firostefani and Imerovigli clinging on to its edges come to sight.

We climb uphill to the track that will lead us to the interior of Nea Kameni where the crater of the volcano is situated. The itinerary through the barren landscape lasts half an hour.

During our walk we reach the northern edge of Mikri Kameni and

In Nea Kameni lies the crater of the Santorini volcano.

From Nea Kameni we can distinguish the coasts of the "lacerated" Santorini and the all white houses of Fira which balance on the edge of the caldera cliffs.

from there the Daphne lava. As we continue, we bypass on our left-hand side the vault of Nike which has a height of 117 meters and on our right-hand side the vault of Fouqué (126 m high), the vault of Rek (on the right, 127,6 m) and on the left the two Smith vaults (127 and 125 meters each). We continue on the track and walk along the edge of the "Twin Stack" where the crater lies until we reach the top of the George I vault, the highest peak on the island, 130,8 meters in height.

The landscape we stare at is strange and weird. Around us big and smaller cavities which used to be craters that hurled out glowing lava and ash, while in some spots hot vapours and sulphur gases emerge, the temperature of which varies and might reach 86C. We feel that the soil is hot while the air is lukewarm and the smell of sulphur diffused in the atmosphere.

As we look at the crater and its inner walls, which are hurtling to the abyss, we are overwhelmed by a feeling of awe for human insignificance in front of the Elements.

Our next station is Palia Kameni. The boat will leave us on a small bay facing Nea Kameni. We will swim between two volcanic islands where the waters are lukewarm (30-35C) and opaque having a greenish and yellowish colour because of the presence of sulphur.

After Palia Kameni the boat heads to Therasia which is a remnant of the western coast of prehistoric Strongyli.

On the edge of the Therasia cliff "unfold" the white houses of its main settlement, Manolas, while lower on the coast the small mooring of Korfos is distinguished.

THERASIA

It lies opposite Oea and has an area of about 16 square kilometers (5,7km in length and 2,7 km in width, in its widest point). Its inhabitants are no more than 200.

We disembark on the small anchorage of **Korfos** with the little white houses, the ship-yards and the ash and stone bollards which were used by boats in the past.

Like in Santorini, one of the island's coasts, the eastern one, falls abruptly into the sea. Around the middle of this coast, on the top of the cliff (160 meters above sea level) lies the main settlement called **Chora** or **Manolas**. Stairs from Korfos lead to the all-white village which, like the caldera settlements in Santorini, balances along the cliff's edge.

In Therasia, as in the villages of opposite Thera, we will see the same

lily-white little houses built next to each other and the same alleys. The only difference between the former and the latter is tourist development. Therasia has not followed Santorini's swift advance. Nonetheless, this fact bestows a special charm upon the island.

After Korfos the boat continues its course parallel to the northeastern coasts of Therasia and reaches the island's newest harbour, Riva, where the little St. Irene church is situated which arguably gave its name to Santorini (See p. 30). From **Riva** an asphalt road leads us after 4km to **Potamos**, the second of the three Therasia villages, which has 90 inhabitants and picturesque hollowed-out houses built in a gully. We continue on the same road and after one kilometer we reach the capital, Manolas, with the small tavernas and the picturesque houses which look clung to the caldera edge and the St. Constantine church which domi-

nates its centre. On the south of Potamos lies the third settlement, the deserted **Agrilia** with the Virgin Mary of Langadi (gorge) church while on the southern part of the island lies the Dormition monastery. Built in the 19th century it faces the caldera, both Nea and Palea Kameni and Santorini in the background. In the centre of the monastery rises the Virgin Mary temple with a unique inlaid with gold iconostasis.

The nature in Therasia resembles that of Santorini. The landscape is characterized by low vegetation. The same terraced fields, where props hold the stony soil. The same crops: vines and vegetables. The same grey and red colour patched by the white of houses and churches. The same view over the dark blue waters of the caldera, while opposite the oblong silhouette of the greatest island of the complex, Santorini, looms together with the white figures of its houses that are hooked on the edge of the precipice. Therasia is the twin little sister of Santorini and therefore the similarities between them abound. In Therasia the western coasts which face the open sea are low with only a few beaches in contrast to the eastern ones which end in the caldera and are high and precipitous. On the southern coast of Therasia, beside the sea lies the Trypiti cave.

Leaving Therasia behind we complete the sailing round of caldera crossing the Passage that separates the two islands. We will make one more stop, at the Oea harbour. Then we will follow the abrupt western coasts of Santorini. As we sail almost parallel to the caldera precipitous walls, we will have the opportunity to observe the variety of colours which distinguishes its rocks until we reach our starting point, Mesa Yalos or Athinios.

Besides Manolas, which faces the coasts of Santorini, Potamos, built in a gully is the second settlement of Therasia.

With the island of Therasia, our acquaintance both with history as well as with the natural beauties of Santorini comes to an end. The island that most of all demands and expects intense feelings. Because it is certain that after getting to know the place, we will love it. Because it is the island which accomplishes the infinite pleasure of travelling and dreaming under the Greek light.

When the sun sets. . .

together with our journey, a day in Santorini comes to an end. It is
the sweetest time of the day. As the sun lowers and light becomes
thinner, Santorini changes. Houses, cobbled-roads, churches, sea,
volcano, caldera look different. Everything is dressed with a golden
veil which becomes deep purple when the sun dives into the
Aegean waters. Every moment offers new colours to the island.
The chain of lights is on. As day gives way to night, new sounds
fill the air.
The day is gone but life goes on in Santorini. Stores are set to life.
People swarm the streets. Tavernas, restaurants, cafeterias, bars,
discotheques and all sorts of night-clubs are packed. Music and

voices take the place of tranquility and serenity which reign in the
dusk, the most romantic time of the day.
Santorini is famous both for its antiquities and natural landscape as
well as for its night-life. It goes on the whole night. And when the
last night-birds leave the clubs and go to sleep the electric lights are
already off and as day breaks, the pale dawn touches the vertical
and concave surfaces of houses and churches. A new day, a new
circle of life for the island.

. . . with our journey a day

in Santorini reaches its end. . .

USEFUL INFORMATION
HOW TO GET TO THE ISLAND

BY AIR

There are daily services from Athens to Santorini. The flight is about 50′. The airport lies 7km from Fira.

For more information you can contact the Olympic Airways agency in Athens and Santorini.

BY FERRY-BOAT

There are daily services from Piraeus to Santorini. Distance from Piraeus 130 nautical miles, journey duration about 8-9 hours. Information at the Piraeus and Santorini Port Authorities.

BY SPEED PASSENGER BOAT

From Rafina which lies 27km east of Athens there are speed boats (catamaran) to Santorini (journey duration about 6 ½ hours).

From Santorini to other destinations...

From Santorini you can travel by boat to the rest of the Cyclades (Amorgos, Anafi, Ios, Kimolos, Kythnos, Melos, Mykonos, Naxos, Paros, Serifos, Sikinos, Sifnos, Syros, Tinos, Folegandros), to some of the Dodecanese and Sporades Islands, to Iraklion in Crete, to Volos and Thessaloniki. Information at the Piraeus and Santorini Port Authorities.

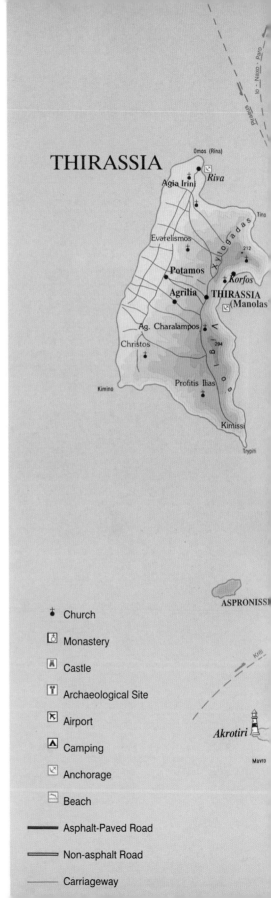

THIRASSIA

Omos (Rina)
Riva
Agia Irini
Tino
Evarelismos
212
Potamos
Korfos
Agrilia
THIRASSIA
(Manolas)
Ag. Charalampos
294
Christos
Kimino
Profitis Ilias
Kimissi
Trypiti
ASPRONISSI
Krili
Akrotiri
Mavro

✝ Church

Monastery

Castle

Archaeological Site

Airport

Camping

Anchorage

Beach

—— Asphalt-Paved Road

══ Non-asphalt Road

—— Carriageway

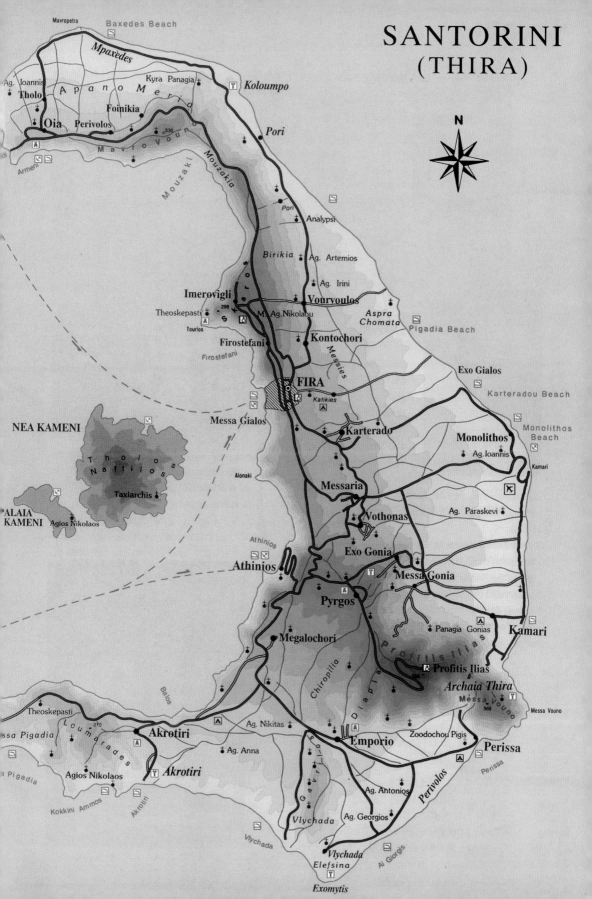

GETTING AROUND THE ISLAND

The road network of Santorini is generally good.

Buses perform daily services to all villages. There are taxis as well as rent-a-car and motorbike agencies while travel agencies in Fira and elsewhere organize excursions to the is-

SPORTS

As for sports in Santorini, you can best enjoy swimming and aquatic sports. Nonetheless, due to the small distances, the island and Therasia alike are also ideal for hiking. If you enjoy hiking you can simply explore the fascinating spots of both islands in your personal manner, early in the morning or late afternoon, at dusk.

If you have a sailing boat you can berth it in Fira bay. For information about supplies and possible repairs you can contact the Santorini Port Authorities.

You can also visit by boat, besides Nea Kameni, Palia Kameni and the hot springs with the greenish and yellowish sulphur waters which lie between the two islands.

land's attractions and archaeological sites.

From Mesa Yalos (or Fira Bay) small boats sail to Nea and Palia Kameni, Therasia (Korfos and Riva) and Oea. From Athinios a ferry-boat sails daily to the same des-

tinations with an extra stop in Mesa Yalos.

During your excursion in Nea Kameni, it is necessary to carry water with you. For your walk from the point that the boat leaves you in Nea Kameni to the crater of the volcano you will need a hat and suitable shoes because the soil around the crater is hot.

YOU MUST ALSO KNOW THAT:

You need suitable walking shoes during your visit to the Ancient Thera archaeological site.

There is a helicopter-port in Manolas, Therasia.

When the ferry-boat reaches Riva in Therasia, if you did not go by your private car there is a bus on hand to Potamos and Manolas.

THERASIA

Therasia is ideal for quiet holidays on a location, which remains serene and picturesque, as it is not yet touched by intensive tourist development.

FOOD AND ENTERTAINMENT

In Santorini and most particularly in Fira, all sorts of restaurants with Greek and international cuisine, ouzeri, tavernas, pizza-, kebab-, snack- and barbecue restaurants are open during the summer. There are also cafés and pastry-shops.

For your nightlife you will find numerous bars and pubs as well as discotheques mostly with foreign music.

From the local traditional cuisine it is worth tasting the famous tomato croquettes made of tomatoes, onions, aromatic herbs and flour, the white aubergines, a kind of cheese called "chloro" and the local sausages.

THE LOCAL CUISINE

Local dishes are frugal as the landscape. They bear the smell and taste of the island. Mint and basil give their aroma, and the humble caper becomes a delicious dish cooked in many different ways. The island's cuisine consists mainly of legumes and vegetables. The principal specialties are the various fried croquettes of vegetables, such as onion or mixed vegetables croquettes.

The most famous of all are the tomato croquettes, which contain tomatoes, mint, flour, onions and sometimes are seasoned with cinnamon. The split peas are a kind of national dish for local people. They are often served with caper cooked by stewing. It is occasionally seasoned with cooked onions. Local housewives invent many variations of dishes with split peas, such as split peas with rice (a kind of soup) or croquettes. The eggplant salad is made of the local white eggplants and is seasoned with caper.

Sausages, called apokti, are made from pork meat, and the favourite fish are fries and horse mackerels, called psarolia, which are left to dry under the sun and are served as snacks.

Stuffed tomatoes, aubergines and peppers, which are to be found throughout Greece, have a special taste because they are cooked without meat and seasoned only with basil and mint.

All the above-mentioned delicacies are accompanied by a glass of wine product of the Santorini fragrant vine and completed by a dessert.

The island's pastries are as simple as its dishes. The sweet-smelling melitinia are made of home-made pastry sheet stuffed with sweet cheese and scented with mastic from Chios. The kopania consist of pounded barley rusks and currants, while the semolina puddings are hangovers of the Venetian occupation.

EVENTS

If you are in Santorini in August, it is worth attending an event (custom) which relates to the island's volcano. It is called the "Awakening of the Volcano" and is an impressive representation of the volcanic eruptions.

SHOPPING

In Santorini as in any other popular tourist resort you will find countless shops with all kinds of objects, souvenirs as well as various folk art objects. Beside these objects you can buy good quality wines (brusco, bordeaux, nychteri and the sweet red visanto), paintings of Greek and foreign artists representing its charming landscapes, hand-woven textiles from the weaving-mill in Oea.

From local products it is worth buying split peas, caper, small tomatoes (which are also made into a sweet) and flavoured with rosewater macaroons.

USEFUL TELEPHONE NUMBERS IN SANTORINI

Area code	22860
Town Hall	22231
Police	22649
Santorini Medical Centre (Fira)	22237
Greek National Tourism Organization (G.N.T.O.)	71234
Port Authority	22239

CLASS	NAME	TEL.	BEDS
AYIOS GEORGIOS EMBORIO (0286)			
A	SABBAS (F.A.)		39
AKROTIRI			
B	ADAMASTOS	81188	42
C	AKROTIRI	81375	30
C	GOULIELMOS	81383	52
ASPAKI OEA			
B	AEGEAS VILLAS (T.F.A)	71466	5
EMBORIO OR NIBORIO			
A	NINE MUSES (B)	81781-7	95
C	PERISSA	81105	102
EXO GONIA			
C	MAKARIOS	31375	82
FIRA			
A	ASTERAS VILLA (F.A.)	22590	14
A	ATLANTIS	22232	46
A	DAEDALUS	22834	54
A	EGIALOS (F.A.)	25191-5	55
A	EL GRECO (F.A.)	24946-7	50
A	EN PLO (T.H.)	24270	20
A	ENIGMA (T.F.A)	24024	12
A	MIKROS HELLENAS (T.F.A)		16
A	SANTORINI PALACE	22771	196
A	VILLA THEOXENIA (T.H.)	23386	12
B	ARESSANA	23900-1	105
B	LOUKAS (T.H.)	22480	33
B	PORTO FIRA (T.F.A.)	22849	28
C	ANTONIA		20
C	HELLAS	23555	33
C	KAVALARI (T.H.)	22455	37
C	KING THERAS	23882-3	32
C	MELINA	22421	34
C	NISOS THERA (F.A.)	23252	19
C	PELICAN HOTEL	23113-4	34
C	PORTO KARRA	22979	29
C	THEOXENIA	22740	20
C	VILLA RENOS	22848	15
C	SUN RISE	24555	41
FIROSTEFANI			
A	NOMIKOS VILLAS (F.A.)	24670-1	14
A	TSITOURAS(T.F.A.)	22760	10
B	SUN ROCKS II(F.A.	23241	19
B	DANA VILLAS III (T.F.A.)	22566	12

CLASS	NAME	TEL.	BEDS
C	DANA VILLAS(T.F.A.)	24641-3	17
C	DANA VILLAS II (T.F.A.)	24641-3	35
C	GALINI	22095	13
C	HERA (F.A.)	23488	19
C	KAFIERIS	22189	20
C	MANOS (F.A.)	22091	29
C	NIKOLAOS KAFIERIS (F.A.)	22059	15
C	SUN ROCKS (F.A.)	23241	13
IMEROVIGLI			
A	AEOLUS VILLAS (F.A.)	23321	15
A	ALTANA APARTMENTS (T.H.)	23240	30
A	CALDERAS APARTMENTS (T.F.A.)	23402	12
A	ILIOTOPOS (T.F.A.)	23670	17
A	ROKA BAY (T.H.)	23569	19
A	STRATOS VILLAS (T.H.)	23889	20
B	ALEXANDROS VILLAS (T.H.)	23124	10
B	ANDROMEDA VILLAS (T.F.A.)	24844-6	16
B	ARTS SANTORINI (T.F.A.)	23258	15
B	GALAXY (F.A.)	22753	15
B	KELYS (T.H.)	24767	6
B	KROKOS (F.A.)	22488	13
B	NEFELIS HOMES (E.Δ.)		12
B	REMEZZO VILLAS (F.A.)	23030	15
B	SKAROS VILLAS (T.F.A.)	23153	13
C	THANOS VILLAS (F.A.)	22883	31
C	HONEY MOON VILLAS (T.F.A.)	23058-9	20
KAMARI			
A	BELONIA VILLAS	31138	41
A	KALLISTI VILLAS (T.F.A.)		22
A	VILLA ANNABELLE (F.A.)	32770	31
A	ROSE BAY	33650-2	81
B	ANTINEA (B)	32753-4	46
B	ARMONIA	32141	49
B	ASTRO	31366	82
B	APHRODITE 2	32760	60
B	GLAROS	31713	49

CLASS	NAME	TEL.	BEDS
B	DELFINIA (F.A.)	33177	41
B	ESTIA		32
B	PLAZA	32976	60
B	RIVARI	31687	72
SANTORINI (H&B)			
B	ROUSSOS BEACH HOTEL	31255	72
B	SELLADA (F.A.)	33090	40
B	STRONGYLI	32802	38
B	CHRISTOS (F.A.)		40
C	ADONIS	31956	43
C	AKIS	31670	36
C	ALKYON	31295	38
C	ANASTASIA		60
C	ARGO	31374	33
C	ARTEMIS BEACH	31198	72
C	AVRA	31910	39
C	KAMARI BEACH	31243	118
C	KAPETAN YIANNIS (F.A.)	31154	30
C	KASTELI	31530	104
C	LEVANTE	31160	80
C	MATINA	31491	52
C	ORION	31182	93
C	POSEIDON	31698	60
C	SIGALAS	31260	79
C	SUNSHINE	31394	68
C	TROPICAL BEACH	32222-3	53
C	VATOS	31660	62
C	VENUS	32760-4	117
C	ZEFYROS	31108	79
C	ZEUS	31473	45
KARTERADOS			
B	ALBATROS	23435	73
C	LONDOS	22146	39
C	NICHOLAS	23912	28
B	SANTORINI TENNIS CLUB (T.F.A.)	22122	22
KATO FIRA			
C	ANTITHESIS (T.H.)	22844	8
MEGALOCHORI			
A	VENTEMA (F.A.)	81796-7	108
A	VILLA DOLPHIN (T.H.)	81663	12
C	SANTORINI STAR	81198	25
MESARIA			
A	ARCHONTIKO ARGYROU	31669	28
A	SANTORINI IMAGE	31874-5	228
B	VOLCANOS VIEW VILLAS (T.H.)	24780-2	98

CLASS	NAME	TEL.	BEDS
C	ANNY	31627	77
C	ARTEMIDOROS	31640	56
C	CALMA	31967	69
C	LOIZOS	31733	23
C	SANTORINI MEMORIES	31918	56
MONOLITHOS			
A	SKORPIOS (F.A.)	33666	55
OEA			
A	ATLANTIS VILLAS (T.F.A.)	71214	58
A	ETHRIO SANTORINIS (T.F.A.)	71040-1	49
A	CHELIDONIA (T.H.)	71287	22
A	GOLDEN SUNSET BILLAS (T.H.)	71001-2	4
A	KANAVES OEA (T.F.A.)	71453	19
A	KANAVES II OEA II (T.F.A.)	71453	7
A	LABETIA VILLAS (F.A.)	71237	20
A	MELACHRINOS (F.A.)		12
A	OEA MARE VILLAS (F.A.)		10
A	PERIVOLAS (T.H.)	71308	38
A	RIMIDA (T.F.A.)	71192	17

CLASS	NAME	TEL.	BEDS
A	STOA (T.F.A.)	71468	10
A	TO SPITI TOU YIANNI (T.F.A.)	71538	13
B	AEGEAS VILLAS I (T.F.A.)	22006	7
B	AEGEAS VILLAS II (T.F.A.))	22006	2
B	ANGELIKI (T.F.A.)	71132	7
B	ARMENI (T.H.)	71439	22
B	IRINI (T.F.H.)		13
B	LAOKASTI VILLAS (F.A.)	71343	37
B	LAOUNDA (T.H.)	71204	35
B	ZOE (F.A.)	71466	11
C	KATIKIES	71401	14
C	FINIKIA	71373	29
C	OEA SUNSET (F.A.)	71490	38
PERISSA			
A	KOUROS VILLAGE (F.A.)	81972-4	36
B	SANTA BARBARA	81534	25
C	AMARYLLIS	81682	49
C	GARDENIA	81424	37
C	BLACK SANDY BEACH	82474	14

CLASS	NAME	TEL.	BEDS
C	PETRA NERA	82009	34
C	THERA MARE	81114	61
PERIVOLAS			
B	SEA VIEW (F.A.)	81899	44
PYRGOS			
C	ZORBAS	25040	59
THERASIA			
B	CAVO MARE		38
VOTHONAS			
A	MEDITERRANEAN BEACH	31167	110
A	VILLA DAMIA	32532-4	92
C	KALISPERIS	31832	48
VOURVOULOS			
B	SANTORINI VILLAS (F.A.)	22036	17

ORGANIZED CAMPING • ORGANIZED CAMPING	
CALDERA VIEW	
Megalochori, Santorini P.C. 847 00	82010
PERISSA	
Perissa, Santorini P.C. 847 00	81343
SANTORINI	
Fira, Santorini P.C. 847 00	22944

NOTE:

There are also D and E class hotels as well as rooms to let.

For information contact the local police.

F. A. = Furnished Apartments

B = Bungalows

H. & B. = Hotel & Bungalows

T. F. A = Traditional Furnished Apartments

T.H. = Traditional Hotel

BIBLIOGRAPHY

Adam (publisher): *Castles and castellia of the Aegean.*

Basiliades, D.: *Pebbles of the Modern Greek Myth.* Athens 1986.

Georgalas, G.: *The creation and evolution of the volcanic complex of the Santorini islands.* *

Danezis, M.: *Santorini.* Athens 1971.

Ekdotiki Athinon (publisher): *History of the Greek Nation.*

Katsipis, F.: *From the chronicle of our plain.* *

Katsipis, F.: *Castellia and their patroness-saint St. Theodosia. Vigles and goulades, shelters.* *

Koumanoudis, I.: *The folk houses and churches of Santorini.* *

Marinatos, N.: *Santorini.* Athens 1977.

Marinatos, Sp.: *Excavations at Thera I & II.* Athens 1968 & 1970.

Melissa (publisher): *Architecture of the Cyclades Islands*

Doumas, C.: *The Frescoes of Ancient Thera,* Athens 1992.

ARCHAEOLOGY review, vol. 2,62 and 67.

Simopoulos, K.: *Foreign Travellers in Greece.*

Note: the articles with the asterisk are contained into the book of M. Danezis, Santorini.